Your
Starter
Kitchen

Your Starter Kitchen

THE DEFINITIVE BEGINNER'S GUIDE TO STOCKING, ORGANIZING, AND COOKING IN YOUR KITCHEN

Lisa Chernick

Tiller Press

New York   London   Toronto   Sydney   New Delhi

TILLER PRESS

Tiller Press
An Imprint of Simon & Schuster, Inc.
1230 Avenue of the Americas
New York, NY 10020

First Tiller Press trade paperback edition April 2020

TILLER PRESS and colophon are trademarks of Simon & Schuster, Inc.

For information about special discounts for bulk purchases,
please contact Simon & Schuster Special Sales at 1-866-506-1949
or business@simonandschuster.com.

The Simon & Schuster Speakers Bureau can bring authors to your live event.
For more information or to book an event, contact the Simon & Schuster
Speakers Bureau at 1-866-248-3049 or visit our website
at www.simonspeakers.com.

Interior design by Jennifer Chung
Cover art and design by Patrick Sullivan

Manufactured in the United States of America

1 3 5 7 9 10 8 6 4 2

Library of Congress Cataloging-in-Publication Data
Names: Chernick, Lisa, author.
Title: Your starter kitchen : the definitive beginner's guide to stocking,
organizing, and cooking in your kitchen / Lisa Chernick.
Description: New York : Tiller Press, 2020.
Identifiers: LCCN 2019046258 (print) | LCCN 2019046259 (ebook)
ISBN 9781982139025 (paperback) | ISBN 9781982139032 (ebook)
Subjects: LCSH: Kitchens—Equipment and supplies. | Quick and easy cooking.
Classification: LCC TH4816.3.K58 C525 2020 (print)
LCC TH4816.3.K58 | (ebook) | DDC 643/.3--dc23
LC record available at https://lccn.loc.gov/2019046258

ISBN 978-1-9821-3902-5
ISBN 978-1-9821-3903-2 (ebook)

CONTENTS

INTRODUCTION

Whether you're living in your first apartment with a group of friends, the first place of your own, or a forever home that you've been working toward for years, it will have a kitchen, and the kitchen is always the center of it all. It's where you'll be alone with your coffee and together with roommates, friends, and family—cooking, eating, and living.

However, if you're reading this book, chances are you are a total beginner when it comes to stocking and cooking in your kitchen. You know that the better equipped your kitchen is to take on the tasks of cooking and entertaining, the better it will be at making you happy, but perhaps you have no idea how to get started.

The good news is: the basics of a well-stocked and smooth-running kitchen are essentially the same for seasoned cooks and culinary novices. *Everyone* needs the basics, and in this book, you'll learn what they are, why you need them, and how to use them—whether your starter kitchen is a tiny shared space, a more "grown-up" kitchen with some extra room for storage and cooking, or a forever home kitchen you're simply too overwhelmed to tackle. Moreover, to make it as simple as possible for you to begin your starter kitchen journey, this book is divided into sections that cover each of these three kinds of kitchens.

The first section pertains mostly to kitchens that may have limited space for storage, prep, and cooking, like a kitchen in a college or postgrad apartment that you may or may not share with roommates. Even if you have a larger kitchen, however, you'll want to read this section if you consider yourself to be an absolute novice when it comes to stocking and cooking in your kitchen. In this section, you can expect to find tips for assembling a baseline collection of *must-have* kitchen gear and pantry essentials, divvying up initial purchases among the people you may live with, creatively organizing food storage space, and managing ongoing kitchen-related expenses. You'll also find the steps to basic and essential cooking techniques as well as several easy recipes that are perfect for beginner cooks who might be working in small spaces.

Building on what the first section covers, the second section of this book speaks to any newbie cook who may have a slightly larger kitchen but might not be settled into their forever home just yet. This section gives you all the info you need regarding additional kitchen gear and a more expansive pantry that you can use in this kind of space, clever storage ideas, more essential cooking techniques, and recipes with which you can flex your newfound kitchen skills. In this section, you'll also find tips for getting the most out of a wedding registry if you have one.

The third section of this book covers all the essentials for stocking and cooking in an even larger kitchen space— one that is likely part of your forever home. If you're working in this kind of kitchen, you may feel overwhelmed with all the possibilities of what you need (and don't need) for this space, but don't fret! This section will help you get smart about long-term kitchen storage and organization, as well as great gear to add, when your space—and maybe even your family—has expanded.

Above all, this book is meant to get your kitchen—whichever one you're in—up and running, and to get you cooking in it. Think of these pages as the foundation you need to go from "Where do I start?" to "Come on over, I'll make us dinner." And after you're done reading it, rather than looking at glossy cookbooks and food magazines just for fun, you'll be deciding which recipes you want to make from their pages. Instead of just imagining cooking for yourself and inviting people over for dinner, you'll be doing it, knowing that you and your kitchen are up to the task.

Note: All cooks are welcome here! The gear, ingredients, and recipes in this book come from my own cooking experience, which is Western leaning, and is merely one way to cook in a world of amazing options. So if the suggested gear or ingredients differ from the ones that are essential to the way you cook, please swap yours in, and join me in the kitchen!

Your Starter Kitchen

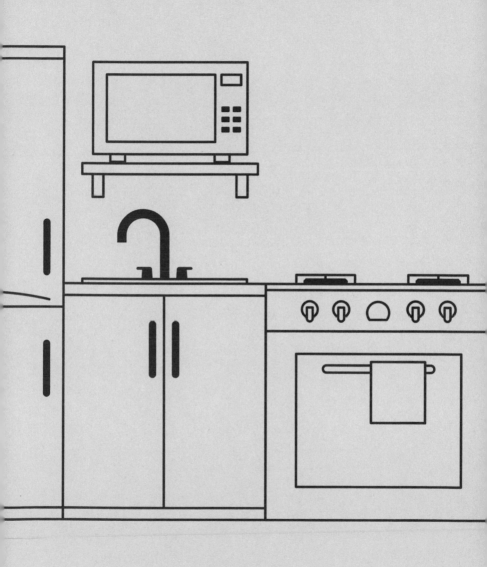

PART 1

FOR A SMALL OR FIRST KITCHEN

Whether you're living in a college apartment you share with roommates or have your own personal kitchen space for the very first time, the prospect of stocking and comfortably working in a potentially small or crowded kitchen may seem intimidating, if not unrealistic—especially if you consider yourself to be challenged in the cooking department. But as this section will teach you, arming yourself with some basic and necessary gear, pantry items, organizational tips, techniques, and recipes will put you in command of your kitchen in no time. It will empower you to make delicious food with confidence, including the world's best granola, a perfect vinaigrette, and single-serve frittatas that you can eat for either dinner or breakfast on the go (the recipes for which are provided at the end of this section). I've also provided a handy checklist at the end of each section that you can mark up and tear out. It includes all of the must-have gear and pantry essentials, so you can keep track of what you have and what you need. These lists make shopping and planning in the brick-and-mortar world or online *soooo* easy. Use them!

MUST-HAVE GEAR

This list of gear for a small or first starter kitchen is not short, but it is a comprehensive rundown of essentials, and you will use these things in every kitchen, always, no matter what! It's the bare-bones list, so to speak. All kitchens will start here and build on this list as your space (and cooking chops!) expands.

- dinnerware
- flatware
- glassware
- mugs
- chef's knife
- paring knife
- serrated knife
- cutting boards

- nonstick pans
- saucepan with lid
- large pot and stockpot with lids
- rimmed baking sheet
- cooling rack
- baking dishes
- large lightweight bowl

- mixing bowls
- measuring cups and spoons
- glass storage containers with lids
- utensil holder
- vegetable peeler
- box grater
- whisk
- wooden spoon
- spatula
- rubber scraper
- spring-loaded tongs
- ladle
- slotted spoon

- offset spatula
- pepper mill
- corkscrew and can opener
- meat thermometer
- salad spinner
- colander and handheld strainer
- muffin tin/ cupcake tin
- coffee maker and kettle
- coffee grinder
- toaster and/or toaster oven
- kitchen linens

In addition to the well-known online and brick-and-mortar shopping options, there are unexpected places to find amazing kitchen gear. The above list includes (but is in no way limited to) thrift stores, outlet shops, estate sales, specialty cookware stores (especially good for testing out and buying knives and specialized gear), restaurant supply stores, homeware giants like IKEA, and family and friends who are looking to downsize. It's also wise to consult consumer review sites when you're narrowing down your options before making a purchase. For affordable cabinet and pantry organization, stores like Target and IKEA are good sources for baskets, bins, and trays in many shapes, sizes, and styles.

DINNERWARE

When it comes to purchasing dinnerware for your starter kitchen, go simple, sturdy, and neutral. Bold patterns and unusual colors may look like fun, but neutral colors are easy to mix and match and you won't mind looking at them at breakfast, lunch, and dinner for years to come. You'll also need plates and bowls in a few different sizes. Consider buying dinnerware in sets, which usually include a dinner plate, a salad plate, and a bowl. Don't spend a lot, as chipping and breaking are par for the course. For a low-level commitment to trendy or clever design, or just to have a few extra plates on hand, try dessert plates—you'll only use them occasionally, so the plates and their appeal will last longer.

FLATWARE (FORKS, SPOONS, AND KNIVES FOR EATING)

Simple and sturdy wins the race here, too. With regard to style, go with your gut. If you love traditional, choose a pattern that skews that way. Do likewise if you have a modern sensibility. Just remember that as is the case with dinnerware, it's best to avoid unusual styles and colors for a primary set of flatware—a few years down the line you might not be that into the look anymore. If you choose flatware that's fairly neutral it will also be easier to replace missing forks and spoons (and they really do go missing—e.g., they accidentally get thrown away) or add more. Flatware is usually sold as sets—a dinner fork, a salad fork, a soupspoon, a teaspoon, and a knife—which generally are an economical option. You also need a set of steak knives if you ever want to eat pork chops, a roast, or of course a steak. You don't need to go high-end, but look for substantial blades that you can imagine using to cut into a piece of steak.

GLASSWARE

Twelve ounces is a good, versatile glass size that you can use for most drinks—from water to iced coffee to even some cocktails. It's also helpful to have both larger and smaller options. A pint glass is great for a beer or a smoothie, for example. Small glasses are nice for juice, and can stand in for wineglasses when you want to be casual. If cabinet space is tight, choose glasses that stack, as stacking can cut your glassware footprint in half. Look for thick, heavy-duty glasses when purchasing your glassware. They will last much longer than anything thin or delicate.

MUGS

As you well know, mugs come in many, many varieties. There are the cool glass double-walled kinds that can be pricey, as well as average mugs that match your dinnerware or have a trendy design or something funny printed on them. All are good. However, unless you love drinking very large quantities of your favorite hot beverage at a fairly fast clip, don't buy oversize mugs. They might look all cozy and cute, but that huge hot coffee will likely get cold long before you can finish it. Plus, giant mugs take up a lot of precious cabinet real estate.

ADDITIONAL KNIVES FOR COOKING

If you were to only purchase one knife to use while cooking in your starter kitchen, make it a **chef's knife**. A good one is an investment, and it will be an indispensable tool that you will use for a lifetime of cooking. When shopping for a chef's knife, look for one that feels balanced and good in your hand, and is built to last. Ideally, buy one at a store that will let you hold the knives you're interested in, so you can feel them in your hand, and even try a few to chop real food. A good knife should feel like an extension of your hand. In terms of size, while a twelve-inch blade is standard in professional kitchens, it would be overkill for home cooks, not to mention intimidating! An eight- or ten-inch chef's knife is ideal for home cooking.

Even though you may be able to get by with just a chef's knife, it is very helpful to have two other knives on hand: a **paring knife** for smaller jobs (think halving cherry tomatoes or cutting the tops off of strawberries) and a **serrated knife** for foods that are hard on the outside and soft on the inside (like a crusty loaf of bread or a bagel). Serrated knives are also excellent for slicing citrus and tomatoes, and for cutting cakes.

If you have a nice knife (or knives), think about where and how to store it in your kitchen. If you plan to keep it in a kitchen drawer, one inexpensive option is a knife guard. It's basically a plastic sheath that keeps the blade in good condition and protects your hands from sharp edges. It also allows you to transport the knife safely if you want to take it to a picnic, for example, or when it's time to move. Knife blocks and magnetic knife holders are also great options. Both will require a bit more of an investment in money as well as effort (installation of the magnetic knife holder) or space (the knife block).

One last consideration is upkeep. To take proper care of your knives, you'll need a steel for honing and a stone for sharpening them. Ask the salesperson at a cookware store to show you how it's done, or look online for video demos.

Tip: If you're shopping for kitchen gear with roommates, split up the pricey, last-a-lifetime items on this list so each person buys and owns whichever sturdy, long-lasting pieces they want, like a great knife or an awesome saucepan. Then share the cost of everything else in whatever way you want. The idea is that someday, when you all go your separate ways, there won't be drama about who keeps the great knife and who gets stuck with the chipped plates.

CUTTING BOARDS

Get two cutting boards: one for raw meat and strongly flavored ingredients like onions and garlic that you plan to cook, and another for fresh fruit and vegetables that you're not going to cook. Here's why: for food safety purposes, even though you can wash a board after using it, it's still better to use a separate board for raw meat, fish, and poultry to avoid cross-contamination of harmful bacteria in raw meats. Taste is also a factor—when you chop garlic and onions, no matter how well you wash the board, traces of those flavors remain. Anyone for a hint of onion in their fruit salad? So, garlic, onions, and meat you'll be cooking go on one board, and fresh produce on another.

Additionally, look for boards with a no-slip feature (which are usually the plastic ones). It's also nice to have one larger board and a smaller one. Some cutting boards even come with a gravy groove, which is great to catch the juices when you're slicing cooked meat or chicken or ripe tomatoes.

In a small space, or in any space for that matter, cutting boards can double as serving trays. Lay a folded sheet of parchment paper on top of the board and voilà, it becomes the perfect platter for cheeses, appetizers, or snacks. Bonus: the parchment paper lends a finished look and makes for supereasy cleanup.

NONSTICK PANS

Nonstick skillets (aka frying pans) and sauté pans are life-savers on the stovetop. To clear up any confusion, a sauté pan has straight sides, and a skillet has curved or slanted sides. These pans are for cooking everything from eggs to asparagus to pork chops, and the nonstick surface makes it so easy, which is why they're good first pans to own. Before you buy, check for restrictions on heat level (some pans are only safe to use on medium-low heat, and no hotter; others can withstand higher heat, which you need for searing or browning food). Having both an eight- to ten-inch pan, for small jobs like frying an egg, as well as a twelve- to fourteen-inch pan so you could make spaghetti carbonara for a crowd, will cover pretty much everything. Stainless steel pans are great, too, but they don't have the ease of nonstick, and high-quality pans can be expensive. Ideally, as you build your kitchen, it's best to have at least one non-stick pan and one heavy, high-quality stainless steel pan. Any pan you choose should also have a lid (for keeping heat and moisture in the pan) and oven-friendly handles. Plastic and wood cannot go in the oven.

SAUCEPAN WITH LID

The ideal saucepan to start with is a small to medium one (two to three quarts). You can use it for cooking rice and grains, making sauces, and steaming veggies. Choose a saucepan that's heavy (stainless steel if possible), with a thick bottom, and you'll have it for life.

LARGE POT AND STOCKPOT WITH LIDS

This could be anything from a six- to eight-quart pot, as well as a larger eight- to twelve-quart, or larger, stockpot, when you can fit it in your kitchen. You'll use these pots to boil pasta, make soup, or cook chili. The larger stockpot comes in handy when you need to boil water for corn on the cob or to make a big batch of beef stock or chicken broth (see page 147, "Making Stock and Broth," in the Large or Forever Home Kitchen section for more about that). Even though quality is always a plus, you can get by with almost anything here as long as it is sturdy with a fairly thick bottom and still relatively lightweight (once you fill this pot, it's going to be heavy!).

RIMMED BAKING SHEET AND COOLING RACK

You are going to do so much with this pan, which is also known as a half sheet. You can use this pan for roasting vegetables, fish, chicken breasts, and sheet pan dinners; making homemade granola; and of course baking cookies (rimless baking sheets are typically the go-to for cookies, but this pan works just fine, too).

Ideally, you should have two of these pans (they stack, so two take up practically the same amount of space as one), because inevitably you'll run out of room on the first one—and there are few things worse than crowding the pan. Doing so will cause your food to steam in the oven rather than brown. When a recipe tells you to arrange the food in the pan in a single layer, take it seriously! And who wants to wait for the pan to free up between batches when you're making cookies?

While shopping, look for heavy, commercial-quality pans that won't buckle even in the hottest oven. They're the perfect size for setting down a precut sheet of parchment paper or a silicone baking mat. Don't bother with non-stick or dark metal options (the nonstick is unnecessary, and dark pans will brown some baked goods too quickly).

Some baking sheets come with wire racks that fit inside. If you have this option, take it. If not, buy at least one **cooling rack with closely set wires**. You'll use it to cool cookies and cakes and for glazing or finishing them.

More Amazing Things You Can Do with a Rimmed Baking Sheet

When you're making pancakes or waffles, set this pan in the oven on low and transfer each batch of finished pancakes to the baking sheet in the oven to keep warm while you finish the rest.

Another nifty use for this pan: if you need to quickly cool down cooked rice or pasta, pour it out onto a rimmed baking sheet, spread it in a single layer, making use of all the pan's surface area, and set it aside to cool. Come back soon, because in a few short minutes that food will be cool.

BAKING DISHES

The two go-to baking dishes for any starter kitchen are the **square pan** (either eight- or nine-inch square is fine) and **the nine-by-thirteen-inch rectangular pan**. Both are versatile and called for often in baking and roasting recipes. Use them to make a cobbler or a casserole, roast a chicken, or even to make a birthday cake. Typically they are available in heavy-duty metal, oven-safe glass, stoneware, ceramic, and porcelain. Choose whatever material you like best, or the best value at the store, as all of these materials will work well. In some cases, these pans (more often the rectangular than the square) are sold with a plastic or metal carrying lid, which makes it easy to safely transport the birthday cake or green bean casserole that you made to the party.

LARGE LIGHTWEIGHT BOWL

Here's a bowl that you will reach for all the time. Picture this: at the bottom of this big, lightweight, attractive bowl you whisk a nice vinaigrette dressing (see recipe on page 58), then you pile on a lot of freshly washed and dried salad greens (see salad spinner on page 19) and gently toss the greens with the dressing, adding more as the greens become sufficiently coated with vinaigrette. Wipe off any messy dressing around the rim of the bowl, then set it out on the table with tongs or a salad server, and you're done.

Or how about popcorn on movie night? Or when you need to whisk batter for pancakes or toss pasta salad for a picnic? This is your bowl for all these things. It should be as large as you can accommodate (remember that you can stack other bowls inside of it to save room), lightweight, and cute. The bowl can be made of aluminum, stainless steel, or enamel-coated metal. Plastic may also be available, but isn't the nicest option for presentation.

MIXING BOWLS

Mixing bowls are usually sold in sets of three or more and are meant to stack. You'll use these kitchen workhorses for prepping food and setting up your *mis en place*—which is fancy French kitchen-speak for ingredients that are cut, measured, ready, and organized for cooking (think sifted dry ingredients when you're baking; or chopped onions, celery, and carrots ready for your soup pot). You can also use these bowls to toss, whisk, and mix everything from guacamole to the filling for an apple pie. Consider buying these in lightweight stainless steel for ease of use and convenience, or glass, which can double as serving bowls and also go into the microwave. Whatever option you choose should be durable and not too expensive.

MEASURING CUPS AND SPOONS

You'll need both dry and wet measuring cups for your starter kitchen because these tools are not interchangeable. A quarter cup of cream and a quarter cup of powdered sugar each need to be measured in a different way, with a different device. The wet measuring cups are usually clear, made of glass or plastic (glass is sturdier and will last longer), have a small spout, and are typically used for water, broth, milk, wine, or any other liquid. They typically come in one-, two-, or four-cup sizes with lines to indicate fractional amounts along the way. Having a one-cup (plus a four-cup, if you have space) liquid measure in the kitchen should meet most needs.

Dry measuring cups are usually made of plastic or metal (although metal holds up better), and are sold in sets—the norm is one cup, one-half cup, one-third cup, and one-fourth cup. Measuring spoons are also a kitchen necessity that you can buy in plastic or metal, and that come in sets with measures for one tablespoon, one teaspoon, one-half teaspoon, and one-fourth teaspoon.

GLASS STORAGE CONTAINERS WITH LIDS

When it's time to store leftovers in the fridge or freezer, and maybe even more important when it's time to reheat those leftovers in the microwave, glass storage is the gold standard. Buy a few round or square stackable containers with lids in a variety of sizes. It's fine to use plastic takeout containers to supplement your storage needs, but avoid using those in the microwave.

> *Tip:* When deciding where to store all of your must-have gear in a compact kitchen, a few helpful rules of thumb are: choose drawers and cabinets near the sink and/or dishwasher to keep frequently used plates, cups, flatware, and utensils. If something is easy to put away after it's clean, you're more likely to put it away! Keep frequently used gear and pantry items at eye level and things you'll only reach for occasionally on the lower and higher shelves. And if your cabinets are tall enough to store baking sheets and cutting boards upright, they're much easier to grab and to store vertically.

COOKING UTENSILS

These utensils make up a great basic set of tools for your starter kitchen, and you can add to this set when you discover what tool(s) you need that you don't have. To save space and stay organized, get a countertop **utensil holder** to fit as many of these as makes sense, and keep them organized and handy near the stove.

A **vegetable peeler** is great for prepping potatoes and carrots before chopping them, peeling apples for pie, cucumbers for salad, zucchini ribbons for sautéing, even shaving cheese and chocolate.

A simple **box grater** is an all-purpose option for finely and coarsely grating everything from citrus zest to cheddar cheese. A **whisk** is great for mixing raw eggs, whipping cream, and combining dry ingredients for baking. A **wooden spoon** (buy two or three of these) is perfect for stirring sauces and pasta, and a **spatula** will lift all your cooked foods up and out of the pan. A **rubber scraper** will help you fold ingredients into a cake batter and then scrape out the bowl. Another must-have utensil is **spring-loaded tongs**, which you'll use for tossing salad greens with dressing, tossing spaghetti with sauce, and moving hot food around in a skillet during cooking. You might find yourself reaching for tongs so often that you will buy an extra set or two. Metal is best.

A heavy-duty stainless steel **ladle** will last forever. You'll use it for stock, soup, and chili. And a **slotted spoon** is what you'll use to lift poached eggs out of the water after they're cooked. It's also great for lifting blanched vegetables from a pot of boiling water. And finally a small **offset spatula**. Yes, I know it may seem like something for advanced bakers, but a small offset spatula is one of those inexpensive tools that is a game changer when you need to spread and smooth batter in a pan, frost any kind of cake or cupcake, and even slather condiments on a sandwich. You'll kick yourself for all the years you used a butter knife to do the jobs this tool was born to do.

PEPPER MILL

A pepper mill won't take up a lot of space or cost a lot of money, and it will deliver something that preground pepper never will: big, bold taste. Before cooking meat or fish (whether you're grilling, roasting, sautéing, or cooking in any other way), you must season it with salt and pepper for a tasty result. And when it comes to pepper, freshly ground is what you want. It releases aromas, heat, and flavor that you might not even know you're missing.

CORKSCREW AND CAN OPENER

Always keep a basic **corkscrew** in the kitchen. The standard-issue waiter's model is inexpensive, will open both beer and wine bottles, and takes up about as much space as a fork. There are other options available, from winged-style openers to lever corkscrews to electric openers at varying prices. It's fine, even wise, to have more than one on hand. As for a **can opener**, get a smooth-edge style. It cuts around the outside of the can, and leaves smooth edges, which is safer.

MEAT THERMOMETER

A meat thermometer is a small, inexpensive gadget that's essential for food safety. Honestly, without one it's very hard to know if a pork tenderloin is cooked to a safe temperature (145 degrees according to the USDA, in case you're wondering) without playing guessing games. Ditto for Thanksgiving turkeys, grilled chicken breasts, and that beautiful filet of beef you spent a fortune on and don't want to cook past medium rare. Without a meat thermometer, all you can do is cross your fingers. After years of cooking those tenderloins, chops, filets, birds, and even burgers, you will learn to tell when they're done by feel without always needing the thermometer, but even then, it's nice to double-check with this tool for reassurance. And it couldn't be easier to use—with an instant-read thermometer, simply push the probe into the thickest part of the meat, without touching bone, and give the thermometer a moment to get the reading. You can can also opt for an ovenproof meat thermometer. It allows you to insert a probe into the meat, and leave the thermometer in the food, inside the oven, until the desired internal temperature is reached.

SALAD SPINNER

Before you zoom past this entry because you're *sure* that a salad spinner is unnecessary—you may think it's a space hog at best and a frivolous gadget at worst—please read on, because there is a serious case to be made in favor of this amazing item. If you ever eat salad, or think you should eat more salad but don't really want to because the task of washing and patting dry the greens is onerous and off-putting, I am with you. But I have come to see the light, and that light is a salad spinner.

This piece of gear is a game changer, and with it you'll be able to prewash greens and stash them in the fridge to enjoy all week long in salads, soups, or sautés, on sandwiches, and to add vegetal crunch to anything. In addition to salad greens, you can use your salad spinner to bathe fresh herbs and gently wash berries without smashing or bruising them. Besides nudging you to eat more healthy produce, the salad spinner's other great gifts are all the paper towels it will save the environment, and the precious time it will save you.

COLANDER AND HANDHELD STRAINER

For your starter kitchen, you really need just one medium-size colander and one medium-size handheld mesh strainer. You'll use the colander to rinse vegetables and fruit, as well as drain pasta and cooked vegetables. **Colanders** come in various materials: plastic, stainless steel, aluminum, and enamel-coated metal, and they usually have little feet or a base so the colander can sit, elevated just enough so its contents don't touch the bottom of the sink.

Handheld strainers are great for rinsing rice, draining a can of beans, or draining yogurt and fresh cheese (ricotta), if you are up for that sort of project. You can also use a strainer for sifting dry ingredients for baking recipes, or draining a few olives or capers to toss onto a salad.

MUFFIN/CUPCAKE TIN

This is another item that might be easy to write off, but you'd be wrong to do that. Obviously, if you're baking muffins or cupcakes, you'll want one of these. But less obviously, if the idea of individual heat-and-go breakfast frittatas, mini meat loaves, or just-for-one mac-and-cheese cups speaks to you, a muffin tin is essential for a starter kitchen, as are the perfectly sized paper or parchment cup liners that eliminate the need to grease the pan, make cleanup a breeze, and lend portability to muffin-tin foods. Many muffin tins are nonstick, but don't necessarily need to be. Many are also dark metal, which will brown some foods and baked goods more quickly. Look for heavier tins when stocking your kitchen, but don't break the bank on this one.

COFFEE MAKER AND KETTLE

If you're a coffee and/or tea drinker, you need one or both of these. You could certainly get by with microwaving water or boiling it in a pot on the stove for tea, but do you really want to? With an electric (or stovetop) kettle making tea is pleasant and enjoyable, and in the case of the electric kettle, also quicker.

As for coffee, if you're drinking it at home, you need to have a coffee maker. You can choose from many types, depending on the kind of coffee you want to make and the price you're looking for. There are electric drip coffee makers and manual pour-over styles—the French press is a well-known version of the latter. Cost ranges from very low to hundreds of dollars. Percolators (very old school!)—both stovetop and electric—are generally inexpensive. Espresso makers range from very inexpensive stovetop models to pricier single-serve pod machines to home versions of the professional machines used at coffee shops that can cost as much as a motorcycle. Decide which type (or types) of coffee you'll make most often at home, what you can spend, and go get caffeinated.

COFFEE GRINDER

Serious coffee drinkers may want to go the extra mile and invest in a coffee grinder. For optimal flavor, buy whole beans and grind them yourself just before brewing. There are different types of grinders, the two main ones being burr and blade (burr being preferred, but it can be pricey). If you choose to go deep into the weeds in your research on these, you'll learn about their unique merits and shortcomings. A good coffee grinder is a piece of gear you will appreciate every morning.

TOASTER AND/OR TOASTER OVEN

If you like toasted bread, bagels, English muffins, or waffles, a toaster or toaster oven is a must. The range in price and style for both is vast—you can get a no-frills, two-slice toaster on the cheap, or a costlier fancy retro-chic four-slice number. If you have more money to spend, a toaster oven (aka a countertop oven) could meet all your toasting needs *and* be quicker and more efficient than a full-size oven when it comes to jobs like broiling a few chicken breasts, warming up leftovers, making nachos, and baking a cake. It's really just a matter of counter space and how much you want to spend, so choose whichever works best for you.

KITCHEN LINENS

Regarding kitchen linens, I'm talking about pot holders and kitchen towels. Whether you're pulling a hot baking sheet out of the oven or grabbing the handles of a pot of pasta off the stove to drain it, pot holders are a must. Kitchen towels are similarly indispensable, and called upon for many jobs beyond drying dishes. Set a basket of warm bread on the table and drape one on top to keep the heat in without the bread going soggy. Stabilize a cutting board and mixing bowl on the countertop during use, or create a makeshift trivet to protect your table from hot cookware you're serving from. They do a lot, so you should have three or four in the kitchen at all times.

A Kitchen Towel Tip for Cooking Rice

As soon as a pot of rice has cooked on the stovetop for the length of time specified on the rice's package instructions, remove the pot from the heat, lift the lid, and set a folded kitchen towel over the top of the pot. Place the lid on top of the towel, and let the rice rest for ten to fifteen minutes. The towel helps absorb and redistribute the moisture in the rice so it's perfectly cooked every time—not too wet or too mushy.

GEAR YOU DON'T NEED TO PURCHASE (AT LEAST FOR NOW)

Unless you are, or are becoming, a serious baker, you don't need a lot of bakeware, especially specialized items like silicone molds, pastry bags, or bread pans.

Avoid single-use utensils like an avocado scooper (which is unnecessary; simply use a spoon).

Don't bother with special gadgets or gear to cook eggs or asparagus, or to snip herbs. Pots, pans, and knives will do the job just fine.

You don't need silicone mats to line baking sheets (parchment paper is just as good or better).

If you are a novice cook, forget about fancy gear. Are you really going to get serious right now about using a pizza stone or sous vide cooking? Probably not.

This list could go on. There is so much kitchen gear on the market—some of it great fun to use, but most of it not essential to setting up a starter kitchen.

ESSENTIAL PANTRY ITEMS

Whether you're in a small, first-time kitchen or your forever home, these basic items should always be on hand so you don't have to run out and shop every time you want to make something. Your kitchen size and cooking abilities may expand, but this streamlined list is the one to come back to in order to always keep your kitchen humming along. And as mentioned in the introduction, basics differ across cuisines, so please use this list as a guideline, and make any swaps you need to tailor it to your cooking.

- olive oil
- neutral-flavored oil
- nonstick spray
- red or white wine vinegar

- distilled white vinegar
- canned and jarred essentials
- dried herbs and spices

- salt (table and kosher) and pepper (or peppercorns for a pepper mill)

- short and long pasta

- rice

- quinoa or couscous

- coffee and tea

- nuts, nut butters, preserves, and sweeteners

- honey and/or agave syrup

- onion

- garlic

- all-purpose flour

- baking soda

- baking powder

- light brown sugar

- granulated sugar

- vanilla extract

- almond extract

- semisweet chocolate chips

- cocoa powder

- oats

- parchment paper

- condiments

- avocados

- lemons and limes

- ginger

- eggs

- plain yogurt

- butter and cream cheese

- frozen necessities

Roommate Relations

If you live with roommates, it can be challenging to divide up the responsibility of shopping and paying for shared items, and then of course everyone needs space for their individual things. Here are some ideas for making room for everyone.

For shared items (and this extends to cleaning and household supplies in the kitchen and bathroom), decide on a shopping and paying plan early on with your roommates, and stick to it. To help keep track of shared items that need to be replaced, try placing a chalkboard or notepad on the wall or fridge, or inside a cabinet, and whoever uses the last of something writes it down so no one is left hanging.

In the name of good roommate relations in shared kitchens, designating storage space for each person will go a long way.

Cabinets: If there's enough room for each roommate to have a cabinet, that makes sharing kitchen space easier. But if there's not, then share the space by using bins and/or labels so you all know whose things are stored where.

Fridge: If you can designate shelves for each roommate, then you don't really need to label anything. But if you share the whole fridge, use bins and label them and/or items. If you don't, be prepared to act cool when you discover that the hummus you were saving for lunch was eaten by a roommate.

Extra storage: For creating extra storage in your shared kitchen space, keep containers or bins handy, along with masking tape and a marker. The bins help staples and personal items stay organized, and the tape and marker make it easy to label it all.

OILS

For your starter kitchen, it's always great to have a bottle of **olive oil** on hand. Find a kind that you like, whether it's buttery, grassy, or spicy (I suggest trying a few to discover the one that suits you), and you'll likely reach for it often when you start cooking—whether you're dressing salads or drizzling on raw and cooked foods as a finishing touch. Nothing beats a drizzle of assertively flavored extra-virgin olive oil and a sprinkle of salt on grilled steak or a platter of sliced fresh tomatoes!

You will also need a **neutral-flavored oil** in the pantry; ideally one with a high smoke point, meaning it can handle high heat without starting to smoke. This is an oil you can use to sauté green beans or fry chicken, as well as use in combination with olive oil to make a perfect vinaigrette (see page 58). Good options for this kind of oil are canola, grapeseed, and vegetable.

Regardless of what kind of oil it is, always store oil in a cool, dark place, and check it for flavor and smell before you use it. After about a year (sometimes more, sometimes less), oils can turn rancid, so trust your nose or tongue to tell you if the oil's gone bad. This is also a reason not to buy oil in large bottles unless you're *sure* you're going to use it.

Last but not least, keep a can of **nonstick spray** (or oil spray) on hand, too. It can help you use less oil when cooking, if you're trying to cut down, and can conveniently deliver a spritz to that one exact spot where you need it.

VINEGARS

Red or white wine vinegar is a good all-purpose choice for salad dressings, to use in cooking, and for drizzling at the end of cooking. Try this: just before serving a pot of lentils, beans, or a hearty soup or stew, swirl in a dash of vinegar. All the flavors will brighten and come into focus.

Distilled white vinegar is good to have on hand as well for pickling, slaws, and even for cleaning up. You can keep a spray bottle of half vinegar, half water handy for cleaning kitchen countertops and spills.

CANNED AND JARRED ESSENTIALS

If you enjoy **tuna**, it's always worth keeping a few cans in the pantry (Spanish or Italian tuna in olive oil is especially good when drained and mixed with fresh lemon juice or red wine vinegar and freshly ground black pepper and salt). Additionally, I recommend keeping a few cans of your favorite **beans** or **chickpeas**, a can of **whole peeled tomatoes**, plus a tube or can of **tomato paste** in your pantry. If you're a fan of **capers** and **pickled jalapeños**, keep those around, too. Any two or three of these items plus a few spices and rice or pasta equals a simple and delicious dinner!

DRIED HERBS AND SPICES

Buy the smallest size container that you can find of any of these spices. Why? Because dried herbs and spices are not meant to last forever. They will lose potency, and when stored for too long, they just don't taste great. In addition to salt (both **table salt** and coarse, flakier **kosher salt**) and peppercorns so you can have freshly ground **pepper**, a solid collection that will serve you well for most basic needs includes **oregano**, **ground cumin,** ground **cinnamon**, **red pepper flakes**, and **bay leaves**. You can always expand the collection, but this is a great starting point for any kitchen, regardless of size.

How to Properly Salt Water for Pasta and Blanching Vegetables

Properly salted water for cooking pasta and vegetables will result in a flavorful finished dish instead of a bland one. After you bring a pot of water to a boil, add a few tablespoons—yes, you read that right, tablespoons of salt. (Keep a box of kosher salt near the stove for this purpose.)

The water should taste like the ocean, so give it a taste. Add a little more if you're not there yet.

When pasta is cooked in properly salted water, it will come out tasting like a food you could eat as is. It will have flavor without tasting salty. Pasta cooked in water that has not been properly salted (or not salted at all) will have no taste. And in turn, any sauce you add it to will fall short. No amount of salt added after cooking can rectify this; the food will only taste salty!

PASTA AND GRAINS

Always keep a supply of **pasta** on hand; having at least one box of long noodles (**spaghetti**, **linguine**, **fettuccine**, etc.) and one box of short (**rigatoni**, **penne**, **farfalle**, **elbows**, etc.) should meet most recipe needs. Whether you opt for plain or whole wheat or any number of the new, ingredient-driven variations such as lentil, rice, or chickpea pasta is up to you. Also, always have a small container of **rice** as well as a box of **quinoa** or **couscous**, too. Any one of these, together with a few other pantry and fridge staples, can help you pull together a meal quickly.

COFFEE AND TEA

If you drink it, it's always worth having fresh **coffee** on hand. Whether you're using whole beans, ground coffee, or pods, make sure you have options on hand. With **tea**, keep an assortment of **herbal**, **black**, **green**, and **chai** loose leaf or bagged teas in your pantry, and you'll be the perfect host. (Or just you can have it for yourself!)

NUTS, NUT BUTTERS, PRESERVES, AND SWEETENERS

Nuts are packed with protein and handily shelf-stable, meaning you can keep them in the pantry or in a cupboard, unrefrigerated. A bag or two of **your favorite nuts** (excellent choices include **almonds, pecans, cashews, peanuts,** and **pistachios**) is a must in any starter kitchen (provided you or anyone you live with aren't allergic). Nuts are great to eat as is, and their richness and crunch are excellent additions to salads, desserts, and granola.

I also recommend keeping your favorite **nut butter** in your pantry, or in the fridge if you don't use it often. Similarly, you should always have a small jar of **fruit preserves** in the cupboard or fridge in case you'd rather have a nut butter and jelly sandwich. **Honey and/or agave syrup,** which is made from a succulent plant, are also essential. They're nice for dipping (hello apples and honey!), for sweetening sauces and dressings, or when you need to sweeten cool foods (think fruit salad) or drinks and don't want to stir and wait for sugar granules to dissolve.

Tip: In general, organizing pantry cabinets using baskets, bins, and trays will be incredibly helpful. Storing like items together (canned goods, baking supplies, oil and vinegar, spices) in containers will go a long way to keeping things organized. And if you have space on the counter, in addition to a utensil holder full of your most-used items, it's also handy to leave out olive oil, salt, and pepper, because you will use them frequently when cooking.

SHELF-STABLE PRODUCE

If you have at least an **onion** and a head of **garlic** on hand, then you have the supporting ingredients you need to cook beans, roast vegetables, or make homemade tomato sauce. Given that you should already have pasta, rice, or other grains in the pantry (see page 33), you could be set to have dinners for days! Best of all, whole, unpeeled garlic and white or yellow onions will last about three months in a cool pantry area.

BAKING BASICS

The urge to bake (or the request that you bring dessert to a get-together) can strike at any time. And it actually takes very little to answer the call. Keep on hand a small bag of **all-purpose flour** (two pounds is plenty), as well as a small container of **baking soda**, **baking powder**, a small box of **light brown sugar**, a small box of **granulated sugar**, a small bottle each of high-quality **vanilla extract** and **almond extract**, a bag of **semisweet chocolate chips**, a small container of **cocoa powder**, and some **oats**, and you will be prepared to make some very nice cookies and brownies and even cakes. (You'll also want to have eggs, butter, and milk in the fridge for this same purpose.)

PARCHMENT PAPER

Parchment paper (on a roll and in sheets) gets its own entry in this book because it really is that fantastic. (Sorry, aluminum foil!) Use it to line rimmed baking sheets pretty much every time you use them—nothing will stick, and cleanup is a breeze. Parchment is also excellent when you're putting together a cheese board or setting out cookies or treats on a platter. Lay a sheet of parchment down first, and everything that goes on top will look a little more polished. Most parchment paper is white, but there are unbleached, chlorine-free versions available as well. If you'd like, you can also look for unbleached parchment paper muffin tin liners.

CONDIMENTS

If you like any of these condiments on burgers, for sandwiches, in dips or dressings, or with breakfast, keep them in the fridge, ready for whenever you need them. Here are some of the top contenders: **ketchup**, **mustard**, **hot sauce**, **soy sauce**, **mayonnaise**, **pickles**, **hummus**, **salsa**, and **maple syrup**.

AVOCADOS

Avocados may be a relatively recent arrival on the starter kitchen essentials list, but if you love to put them on everything, you need to always have one in the kitchen. Slice or dice it into salads, smash some onto toast, or turn it into the best dip of all time: guacamole! See page 48 for the simplest, best way to make it.

How to Choose the Perfect Avocado

More important than color, the key to choosing the perfect avocado is to feel it for ripeness. If you hold it in your hand, a ripe, ready-to-eat avocado will be firm but will yield to gentle pressure. Avoid any that feel mushy or have dark blemishes on the skin.

Ripe avocados should be eaten within a day or two. If you're buying avocados to use in four or five days, choose firm ones instead (four or five days is how long it takes unripe avocados to ripen at room temperature). If they're ripening more quickly than you want, put them in the refrigerator to slow down the process.

To speed up ripening, place avocados in a brown paper bag at room temperature and start checking on them after two days. If you want to supercharge this process, put an apple in the bag with the avocados. The apple gives off ethylene, a natural plant hormone that promotes ripening.

LEMONS AND LIMES

Lemons and limes are both useful and wonderful for different things, so keep a few of each fresh in the crisper of your fridge. You'll be ready to put the finishing touch on a taco (limes), punch up the flavor of a soup (lemons), and make a refreshing cocktail (lemons and limes) whenever you'd like.

Both are also great for squeezing onto fresh fruit in order to keep it from oxidizing and to add a little pop of acidity. These citrus fruits' outermost skin (the zest) is also an essential flavor in sweet and savory cooking—from baking to sauces, slaws, and salads. Whole lemons and limes will last two to four weeks in the fridge before starting to shrivel, get dark spots, and go bad.

GINGER

This knobby little root is packed with warmth and flavor and is a key element in many sweets and desserts, as well as in Asian dishes including stir-fries and dipping sauces. Ginger also makes a nice addition to cocktails and teas and is thought to help soothe an upset stomach. Its outward appearance may look a little intimidating, but all you need in order to peel it is a teaspoon. Simply scrape the edge of the spoon across the skin of the ginger (including the little knobs) and it will come right off. From there, you can slice, chop, or grate it. Whole, unpeeled ginger can last a month in the fridge.

EGGS

What more can I say about eggs besides they are perfect? A food unto themselves, they are a key ingredient in countless dishes. If you have eggs on hand, you can always have a meal. Poach them to eat on toast or on top of a salad, and let the rich yolk become the dressing. Hard cook them for egg salad; scramble them; fry them; make them into an omelet, a soufflé, frittata, fried rice, egg drop soup; place them on top of a burger; or tuck them into a sandwich. Most recipes call for large eggs, which are the best to keep in the fridge (and they last for weeks, so it's easy to store them there).

PLAIN YOGURT

With plain yogurt in the fridge, you can whip up a sauce to serve with fish (just stir in a squeeze of fresh lemon juice, a little mustard, some salt, pepper, and fresh herbs), another sauce for fruit (this time whisk in lemon juice, a little honey, and cinnamon), or just have the yogurt for breakfast with berries and granola. Besides being available in different fat content options (nonfat, low fat, whole), there is also Greek yogurt, which is thicker than regular yogurt and has a creamier consistency.

BUTTER AND CREAM CHEESE

It's good to have more than one kind of butter in the fridge. A spreadable butter is nice on toast (spreadable butter is butter that's been whipped with some oil—usually either canola or olive oil). Unsalted butter is good to use in recipes.

Keep a stick or two in the fridge and another stick or two in the freezer. Spreadable cream cheese is also handy if you like it on bagels or toast.

FROZEN NECESSITIES

Freezers have a way of filling up on their own with leftovers, ice packs, those burgers you didn't get around to cooking, ice cream, and ice cubes. So reserve a little freezer real estate for these kitchen helpers you'll be glad to see. A bag of **frozen berries** is great for making smoothies, or a quick sauce to go over cake or ice cream. A bag of **frozen peas** can be used a little at a time, whether you toss some directly into a pasta dish or add some to soup at the end of cooking. That bag of peas will also make the best-ever ice pack; just make sure to throw out the peas after you've used them for first aid—once they've thawed, even partially, they are not okay to eat.

Bread freezes (and thaws) beautifully. If you like to make yourself the occasional sandwich or toast an English muffin, *the* best way to preserve those baked goods' freshness is to freeze them as soon as you get them home. You're essentially catching the bread at peak freshness and holding it there until you're ready to eat it. Thaw a slice or two of frozen bread on the countertop in half an hour, or leave it overnight (wrap it in a paper towel, kitchen towel, or foil), or toast it and eat right away. While the same method also works for a big, delicious loaf of bread or a long baguette, you can also heat whole loaves in a 325-degree oven for about twenty to thirty minutes to fully thaw and soften them.

TECHNIQUES AND PRIMERS

If you haven't done much cooking, the best place to jump in is with some good basics. And don't equate basic with boring! Think of these ideas as delicious building blocks. Eggs cooked properly are a revelation. Roasting a pork tenderloin and vegetables for dinner can be simple and delicious, or as fancy as you want. Homemade guacamole is the party trick that keeps on giving, and knowing how to make yourself something quick, healthy, and excellent for breakfast is the epitome of self-care. Once you've mastered these skills, you can add to them in lots of different ways, and you'll be ready to take on new ones.

EGGS 101

Many people think cooking eggs is so easy and obvious that no instructions are needed, but they are mistaken. Cooking eggs correctly takes know-how. So if you are a newbie cook, here are some important basics to set you up for success with some of the most popular egg cookery.

Whatever way you cook them, be sure to use fresh eggs! If you're unsure about your eggs' freshness, here's an easy and reliable way to check: submerge an egg in a bowl of water, and if it sinks to the bottom and lies on its side, that means it's fresh. If it sinks in the water and stands on one end, it's still okay to eat, but now's the time to thoroughly cook and eat it. If the egg floats, that means it's gone bad and you need to throw it out.

HARD COOKED

With firm whites and fully cooked yolks, these are the eggs to use for egg salad and deviled eggs. To cook them perfectly, without a greenish layer around the yolk, here's what you do:

Gently set the desired number of eggs in a saucepan so they fit in a single layer.

Cover with lukewarm water, by at least an inch or two, set the pot on the stove, and bring the water to a boil.

Keep an eye on it, and as soon as the water boils, lower it to a simmer and let it go for three minutes.

Turn off the heat and let the eggs sit in the water for ten minutes.

Drain and rinse with cool water until the eggs are cool enough to handle. At this point you can peel and/or store them in the fridge.

SOFT BOILED

These are nice on toast or eaten in an egg cup with a small spoon and salt and pepper to sprinkle on as you go. Similar to a poached egg, the white will be cooked and the yolk will be runny. How runny is up to you, and depends on how long you cook it. Here's how it works:

Bring a pot of water to a boil, then lower it to a simmer.

Add the egg to the water, then start your timer. Five minutes will give you a runny yolk. For a firmer, but still soft yolk, give it seven minutes.

Remove egg with a slotted spoon.

Place the egg in an egg cup or on a work surface and gently tap all around the top with the edge of a knife.

Remove the top and scoop out the egg.

POACHED

Set one of these on top of a salad or a bowl of greens and grains, and you've got a meal. To poach eggs:

In a saucepan, bring two to three inches of water to a boil, then lower the heat to a gentle simmer.

Gently crack one egg one at a time onto a saucer or into a small cup.

Hold the cup close to the water, carefully tipping it and letting the eggs slide into the water.

Simmer the eggs for three to five minutes without stirring or touching the water. The whites should be completely set and the yolks cooked to your desired level of runny.

Lift from water with a slotted spoon and serve.

SCRAMBLED

The longer you cook scrambled eggs, the drier they will become. Keep this in mind and stop the cooking process just shy of the doneness you like. The eggs will cook a little more and firm up after they're off the heat.

The basic method is to:

Whisk together (in a small bowl) a few large eggs with a little salt and pepper and a teaspoon or two of water.

Melt a teaspoon of butter in a heavy skillet or nonstick pan and then pour the eggs into the skillet, turning the heat to low.

Stir the eggs gently as they cook and have nearly reached your desired degree of doneness.

Then turn off the heat and serve.

OMELET STYLE

Follow the method above for scrambled eggs through the point when you pour the eggs into the skillet. But instead of pouring them in and stirring, pour them in and leave them to set a bit. As the edges begin to look cooked, lift them up a little with a spatula and let the raw egg run underneath. When the bottom looks cooked but there is still a little gloss of wet egg on top, you can add grated cheese, fresh herbs, cooked vegetables, meats, whatever you like. Let the ingredients warm through, and then fold the omelet in half and slide it out of the pan. And if it falls apart, it will still be delicious. You can call it a scramble.

ROASTING VEGETABLES AND MEATS

The key to roasting vegetables and meats is to have high heat and plenty of room in the pan for that heat to circulate and cook the food so it's browned on the outside and tender on the inside. A good temperature for roasting is 425 degrees, and if your oven has a convection setting, use it (convection is basically when the oven uses a built-in fan to blow the hot air around inside the oven and cook food more quickly).

There are countless recipes you can use for roasting, but you can never go wrong with this simple method:

Toss **vegetables** that have been washed and dried and cut into same-size pieces, including mushrooms that have been wiped off and either halved or separated into sections if they grow in clusters like maitake or oyster, in a large bowl with a generous drizzle of **olive oil** and a big pinch or two of **salt** and **pepper**. Tip them out onto a rimmed **baking sheet** that you've lined with **parchment paper**, and make sure they're in a single layer. Depending on the vegetable and how small you've cut it, it could be done in as little as ten to fifteen minutes. Start checking asparagus after ten minutes, green beans after twenty minutes, cauliflower florets and mushrooms after twenty-five minutes, and potato wedges after thirty minutes. You want the vegetables to have nice color and be able to be pierced easily with a fork or knife.

Roasting fish fillets or chicken breasts or pork tenderloin is almost the same as roasting vegetables. Drizzle the **protein** with a little **oil** and then sprinkle it all over with **salt** and **pepper**. Set it on a **parchment-lined baking sheet** or in a baking dish where it's not crowded, and slide it into the oven. Fish fillets are done when they're opaque in the middle, chicken when the internal temp is 165 degrees, and pork at 145 degrees. Serve these simple roasted proteins with a sauce on the side, or look for recipes with more elaborate preroasting preparations.

PERFECT GUACAMOLE

Here's a streamlined method for the easiest, most delicious guacamole. First, in your food processor pulse (or use your chef's knife and cutting board to chop) the following: 1 bunch of **cilantro** that you've thoroughly rinsed and dried in your salad spinner, 1 **garlic** clove, one-half to one fresh **jalapeño**. (Test the jalapeño's heat by cutting it and touching the cut flesh with the tip of your finger. Now tap your finger on your tongue, and you'll get a read on the pepper's heat level.) When chopping and handling hot peppers, it's wise to wear gloves, and be careful not to rub your eyes. Know that the seeds in particular pack a concentration of heat, so remove them carefully. Add as little or as much jalapeño as you like according to your preference for heat, juice of two to three **limes**, and **salt**—start with half a teaspoon and go from there. You want this mixture to taste strong and potent, with a good balance of spicy, salty, and acidic flavor. Add additional jalapeño, lime juice, and salt as needed.

In a large bowl, mash three ripe avocados (either a fork or your clean hands are the best tool for this!) to a consistency that's slightly chunkier than you want your finished guacamole to be. Add the herb mixture, a few spoonfuls at a time, mixing and tasting as you go, until you arrive at perfectly flavored guacamole. You may need to add a little extra salt, lime, or jalapeño individually to make it just right.

OVERNIGHT OATS FORMULA

A new classic, this winning breakfast idea is easy to make, healthy, delicious, and portable (if you set it up in a lidded jar or portable container). The basic idea is that you stir plain old-fashioned oats with liquid (e.g., milk, yogurt), plus a few additions of your choice for flavor and texture, and leave it overnight in the fridge. The next morning, you've got breakfast! Give it a quick stir and add a little fresh fruit and/or something crunchy on top, and you're done. Here's the basic formula:

Into a small, deep bowl or jar with a lid, add one-half cup of **old-fashioned oats**, one tablespoon of **chia seeds**, three-fourths cup **milk** (dairy or nondairy) **or** regular (not Greek) **yogurt**, a few teaspoons of **sweetener** (such as maple syrup, honey, or sugar), a pinch of **cinnamon**, and (this last one is super important) a pinch of **salt**.

Give it all a good stir, cover, and refrigerate overnight or up to two days.

Before eating, stir again, and add any toppings you like. You can also add a tablespoon of nut butter and swap the chia seeds for something else, or leave them out altogether.

RECIPES

Much like the primers and techniques for first-kitchen cooks, these recipes are meant to be straightforward and approachable. They're also meant to be adaptable so once you get the hang of them you can start imagining how the recipe might taste with some substitutions—cashews in place of almonds, broccoli instead of green beans—you get the idea. You'll start reaching for the gear you know is ready and waiting, and using it with pantry staples and a few extras, to start making breakfasts, lunches, and dinners. When you cook for yourself you know exactly what you're eating, so not only will you be having food that tastes great, but it will also be healthy, and you'll be empowered by cooking it. As for these recipes, in addition to the gear listed, all of them will use pantry and/or fridge staples and kitchen linens.

SHEET PAN GRANOLA

Makes: about 7 cups   **Total time:** 35 minutes
Gear: measuring cups and spoons, saucepan, large bowl, wooden spoon, sheet pan, parchment paper

This tastes so much better than store-bought granola. It's a great snack, and is amazing with fruit and yogurt for breakfast, or crumbled on top of vanilla ice cream for a knockout dessert.

Ingredients:

3 cups old-fashioned rolled oats

1/2 cup blanched slivered almonds

1/4 cup pepitas (pumpkin seeds), roasted or unroasted

1 tablespoon chia seeds

1/3 cup light brown sugar

1 teaspoon ground cinnamon

1/2 stick (2 ounces) unsalted butter or 1/4 cup coconut oil

1/4 cup maple syrup

1 teaspoon vanilla extract

Scant 1/8 teaspoon almond extract

1 teaspoon kosher salt

Directions:

Position a rack in the center of the oven and preheat to 325°F. Line a rimmed baking sheet with parchment paper.

In a large bowl, combine the oats, almonds, pepitas, chia seeds, sugar, and cinnamon. In a small saucepan, melt the butter (or coconut oil), maple syrup, vanilla extract, almond extract, and salt, stirring to dissolve the salt. Pour over the oat mixture and toss to combine.

Pour the mixture out onto the lined baking sheet, and spread it into an even layer. Bake for 15 minutes. Rotate the pan and bake 10 minutes more, or until the granola is golden. Remove it from the oven and allow it to cool completely (it will crisp up as it cools).

Break the granola into chunks and store in an airtight container for about one month.

MUFFIN TIN FRITTATAS

Makes: 12 frittatas   **Total time:** 35 minutes
Gear: muffin tin, mixing bowl, whisk, heatproof glass
measuring cup, parchment muffin tin liners

It's nice to know that the same piece of gear that gives
you cupcakes can also deliver a healthy breakfast. Store
these frittatas in the fridge for a workweek's worth of
easy grab-and-go breakfasts. They reheat easily—just
pop one into the microwave on high for 15 to 20
seconds and you'll be on your way. Freeze any extras
you know you won't get around to eating. (You can
microwave them directly from the freezer—they'll take
about 45 seconds.)

Ingredients:
5-ounce container
baby spinach or baby kale

Salt and freshly ground
black pepper

12 large eggs

1/4 teaspoon red
pepper flakes

1/2 cup water

6 ounces feta, crumbled

Directions:

Preheat oven to 375°F. Fill 12 muffin tin cups with parchment or paper liners. Place baby spinach in a large microwave-safe bowl and heat it on high for 30 to 60 seconds, or until it begins to wilt. Add a pinch of salt and pepper; toss, and set it aside to cool slightly. Divide the spinach evenly among the muffin tin cups.

In the same bowl you used for the spinach, add the eggs, 1/2 teaspoon of salt, and a pinch of both peppers, and thoroughly whisk or beat the eggs. Transfer the eggs to a spouted pouring device such as a glass 4-quart liquid measuring cup, add about 1/2 cup water so you have 3 cups of egg mixture, and then slowly fill each muffin tin cup almost to the top. Top with crumbled feta, dividing it evenly among the muffin tins.

Bake until cooked through and starting to turn golden, about 25 minutes. Remove from oven (the eggs will have puffed up in the oven, and will deflate as they cool). Cool completely, then transfer to an airtight container and store in the refrigerator for up to 5 days or in the freezer.

CHOCOLATE CHIP PAN COOKIES

Makes: 16 squares   **Total time:** 30 minutes
Gear: 8-inch square baking pan, measuring cups and spoons, mixing bowls, portable mixer or stand mixer

When you keep baking basics in the pantry, you can whip up a batch of these without even going to the store. Perfect for an impromptu get-together or to make for someone.

Ingredients:

1 stick (4 ounces) unsalted butter, softened, plus extra for greasing pan

1/4 cup granulated sugar

1/3 cup brown sugar

1 large egg

1 teaspoon vanilla extract

1 cup all-purpose flour

1/2 teaspoon salt

1/4 teaspoon baking powder

1/4 teaspoon baking soda

3/4 cup chocolate chips

3/4 cup whole roasted peanuts (or hazelnuts or your favorite nut or no nuts at all if you're not nuts about nuts!)

Directions:

Preheat oven to 375°F and butter an 8-inch square pan.

In a medium bowl, beat the butter and both sugars until fluffy, about 1 minute.

Beat in the egg and vanilla. Then add flour, salt, baking powder, and baking soda; mix until just combined. Fold in chocolate chips and nuts.

Press dough into prepared pan.

Bake for 15 minutes, or until golden brown.

Cool in pan; when completely cool, slice into 16 squares and serve.

EASY VINAIGRETTE

Makes: 1/3 cup   **Total time:** 8 minutes

Gear: knife, cutting board, measuring spoons, mesh strainer, pepper mill, whisk, medium bowl

The combination of the two oils creates the balanced flavor that makes this vinaigrette so versatile. The trick of rinsing the shallots and adding a bit of warm water comes from New York City restaurant Via Carota, as reported by Samin Nosrat of the *New York Times,* and it's a vinaigrette game changer! This recipe makes enough dressing for one very big salad, or several smaller ones. Keep unused dressing in a covered container in the fridge, where it will last for a week.

Ingredients:

1 teaspoon minced shallot

1 large garlic clove,
cut in half

1 tablespoon white wine vinegar, plus additional as needed

1 teaspoon warm water

1 teaspoon Dijon mustard

2 tablespoons extra-virgin olive oil

2 tablespoons neutrally flavored oil, such as canola or grapeseed

Generous pinch each of salt and freshly ground black pepper

Directions:

Place the minced shallot in a small mesh strainer and rinse it with cold water. Drain well. Rub the cut sides of the garlic clove all over the bottom and up the sides of a medium bowl. Add the rinsed shallot, vinegar, and warm water to the bowl. Let it rest for a few minutes, then whisk in the mustard, oils, and salt and pepper to taste; adjust salt, pepper, and vinegar if necessary. If the bowl is moving around a lot while you whisk, place a dish towel underneath it to help stabilize it. Serve, or cover and refrigerate.

SHEET PAN "PESTO" POTATOES AND GREEN BEANS

Makes: 4 servings   **Total time:** about 1 hour
Gear: baking sheet, parchment paper, measuring spoons, knife, vegetable peeler, pepper mill, cutting board, large bowl, tongs

An easy side dish that tastes like summer and is great with whatever main course you're grilling or pulling out of the oven.

Ingredients:

2 tablespoons pine nuts

1 1/2 pounds new or baby potatoes, scrubbed and cut in half

12 ounces green beans, trimmed

2 tablespoons olive oil

1 teaspoon salt

1/2 teaspoon freshly ground black pepper

2 ounces Parmesan, shaved with a vegetable peeler

1 bunch of basil, washed and torn or roughly chopped

Directions:

Preheat the oven to 350°F. On a rimmed baking sheet lined with parchment paper, toast the pine nuts—about 10 minutes. Remove from oven and transfer to a plate to cool. Increase heat to 425°F.

Toss the potatoes and green beans in a large bowl with oil and the salt and pepper. Spread evenly on the same parchment-lined baking sheet. Roast, tossing once or twice, until the potatoes are tender and golden and the green beans are tender and browned in spots, about 35 minutes.

Remove from oven, let rest 5 minutes. Scatter Parmesan, toasted pine nuts, and basil on top, and serve.

CHECKLIST FOR A
SMALL OR FIRST KITCHEN

Here's a handy checklist that you can mark up and tear out. It includes all of the must-have gear and pantry essentials for a small or first kitchen, so you can keep track of what you have and what you need. I hope this list will make shopping and planning easy.

GEAR

- dinnerware
- flatware
- glassware
- mugs
- chef's knife
- paring knife
- serrated knife
- cutting boards
- nonstick pans
- saucepan with lid
- large pot and stockpot with lids
- rimmed baking sheet
- cooling rack
- baking dishes
- large lightweight bowl
- mixing bowls
- measuring cups and spoons
- glass storage containers with lids

- utensil holder
- vegetable peeler
- box grater
- whisk
- wooden spoon
- spatula
- rubber scraper
- spring-loaded tongs
- ladle
- slotted spoon
- offset spatula
- pepper mill

- corkscrew and can opener
- meat thermometer
- salad spinner
- colander and handheld strainer
- muffin and cupcake tin
- coffee maker and kettle
- coffee grinder
- toaster and/or toaster oven
- kitchen linens

PANTRY ITEMS

- olive oil
- neutral-flavored oil
- nonstick spray
- red or white wine vinegar
- distilled white vinegar

- canned and jarred essentials
- salt (table and kosher) and pepper (or peppercorns for a pepper mill)
- dried herbs and spices
- short and long pasta

- rice

- quinoa or couscous

- coffee and tea

- nuts, nut butters, preserves, and sweeteners

- honey and/or agave syrup

- onion

- garlic

- all-purpose flour

- baking soda

- baking powder

- light brown sugar

- granulated sugar

- vanilla extract

- almond extract

- semisweet chocolate chips

- cocoa powder

- oats

- parchment paper

- condiments

- avocados

- lemons and limes

- ginger

- eggs

- plain yogurt

- butter and cream cheese

- frozen necessities

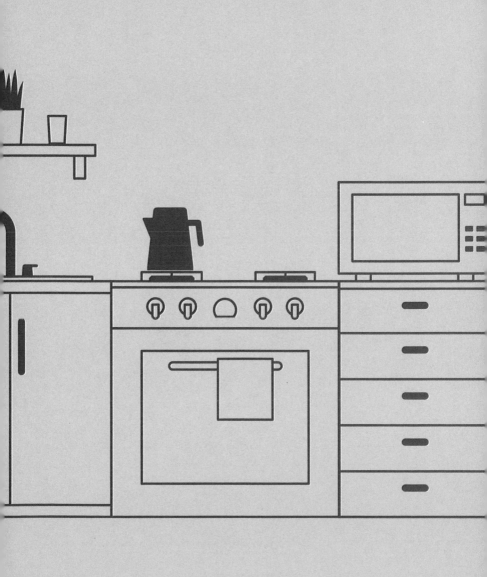

PART 2

FOR A MORE GROWN-UP KITCHEN

This section will help you gather the gear you need, and expand your pantry arsenal, to get you excited about cooking impressive food in a more spacious kitchen (that you don't have to share with roommates!). In addition to the absolute basic gear listed on page 3, you'll bring in more pots and pans, maybe a food processor, and some nice wineglasses, to name just a few things. (If you're looking for tips on the best items for your wedding registry, check out page 80.) You'll also up your cooking game by adding pantry and fridge items that in the past you might've considered aspirational or for restaurants only. News flash: they're not! Last, you'll learn cooking techniques and recipes that are perfect for making in this kind of kitchen. Soon you'll be cranking out party snacks and grown-up dinners, setting up smoothie bowls, and baking pumpkin bread. And if this kitchen isn't quite as spacious as you need it to be, there are plenty of suggestions for space-saving storage and organization in this section, too. Read on!

ADDITIONAL GEAR

In the first section, you received a list of must-have basic gear. The items listed in this section complete your kitchen. This is your 2.0 list of basics, so you're properly equipped to accomplish most any cooking project you want to try. No more "I can't make that recipe" moments because you don't have the right size pan or a cheese grater— the rasp grater will be right there in the drawer! As you consider trying new recipes, you'll know instantly that you've got this.

- handheld electric mixer

- blender and food processor

- kitchen shears

- handheld mandoline-style slicer

- potato masher or ricer

- rasp grater

- handheld citrus juicer

- cake and pie pans

- lasagna pan

- stainless steel and/
  or enameled cast
  iron cookware and
  Dutch oven

- wineglasses and
  bar glasses

HANDHELD ELECTRIC MIXER

Hand whisking has a certain romance to it, and is a nice workout for your arms. That said, as soon as you have the space, a handheld electric mixer will get the job done faster and, in most cases, better. It's inexpensive, and now your cake batter and buttercream frosting can come together in a snap, and you can make a nice bowl of whipped cream without muscle fatigue.

BLENDER AND FOOD PROCESSOR

It might seem like overkill to have both a blender *and* a food processor, but they accomplish different food prep tasks. You can of course get just one or the other, but eventually you may find that both add a lot to your cooking.

You'll love having a blender to make smoothies, frozen cocktails, and milkshakes—and that may be reason enough to have one. But the cool thing about a blender is that it can also puree soups, make a sauce, emulsify a dip, and whip up salad dressing beautifully. Blenders do well with liquids, and excel at delivering smooth, silky results. They get the job done by the force of their motor (not so much their blades, which are not sharp the way a food processor's blades are). The main difference in blender prices (which go from very affordable to wildly expensive) speaks to the strength and quality of that motor. The carafe should be glass, rather than plastic. Glass will hold up much better over time.

A food processor has supersharp blades and a strong motor, and can slice and shred vegetables for beautiful salads and slaws, like the Brussels sprouts recipe on page 112. It can also knead dough for bread and pie crust, and chop nuts beautifully. If you want to break down meat or fish for the freshest ever burger, or shred lots of cheese, the food processor is the multitasker for you. It can also create dips very nicely and make a killer pesto. The only downside of this great tool is that it's not cheap, so feel free to hold off on buying one until you can comfortably afford it.

KITCHEN SHEARS

When you've roasted a whole chicken (or bought a rotisserie chicken), and want to serve it cut up, maybe alongside or on top of a platter of delicious rice or some other side dish, the most efficient way to do so is to cut it with a strong pair of kitchen shears. They're handy for cutting anything food related. It's also much nicer to have a dedicated pair of scissors for food than to use the same ones you use for cutting open packages or making art projects.

HANDHELD MANDOLINE-STYLE SLICER

The deadly serious French and Japanese standing versions of this tool are truly excellent but can feel like overkill to many home cooks (washing and drying them with those razor-sharp blades can be intimidating, too). The hand-held version of this tool is smaller and friendlier, and can be a great addition to your kitchen. Use it to shave all the best things paper thin, from fennel to citrus to root vegetables.

POTATO MASHER OR RICER

Mashers and ricers make the best mashed potatoes! A masher will take up less room, but a ricer will give you the fluffiest final product.

RASP GRATER

Originally a smoothing tool for woodworkers, this simple, handheld grater (now made for cooks) is incredible for zesting citrus, as well as grating ginger, garlic, and hard cheeses into light, fluffy piles. Its teeth are incredibly sharp, though. Most models come with a protective cover, so use it!

HANDHELD CITRUS JUICER

When you need to juice a few limes, lemons, or oranges, this is your go-to gadget. A hinged model is easy to use, extracts loads of juice from the fruit, and can be tossed into the dishwasher for easy cleanup. Stainless steel is ideal because it will hold up best to endless runs through the dishwasher, and last the longest.

CAKE AND PIE PANS

In addition to a **nine-by-thirteen-inch baking pan** and an **eight- or nine-inch-square pan**, both of which you may already have, the following are nice additions to your baking collection.

For all of these pans, look for heavier (rather than lightweight) metal, which is best at conducting heat, with a light-colored finish, which allows crusts to brown nicely but not too fast, which can happen with darker colored pans.

If you want to make cheesecakes, tarts, pound cake, or a Bundt cake, these all have their own dedicated pans— **springforms**, **fluted tart rings** with removable bottoms, **loaf pans**, which are also important for quick breads and meat loaf, and **Bundt pans**, respectively. You don't have to buy these ahead of actually needing them, but when the time comes and you can seek out something other than what's in the supermarket housewares aisle, here are a few tips.

You can use springform pans for cheesecake, flourless chocolate cake, deep-dish pizza, and ice cream cake. These pans consist of a round, flat base and a circular metal belt with a latch that opens to allow the cake to be unmolded and served. Helpful features in a springform include a base that extends an inch or so wider than the pan's collar, so you have something to grab if you need to move the pan when it's in the oven. It also helps, at least a little, to keep liquids from leaking out of the pan.

A **pie pan** (sometimes called a pie plate) is needed for

making pies and quiches, and can also be employed to bake other things like a chicken breast or two, or a piece of fish. Typically either eight, nine, or ten inches in diameter, pie pans are available in ceramic, oven-safe glass, aluminum, and nonstick, and come in regular depth (one to one and a half inches) and deep dish (two to two and a half inches).

LASAGNA PAN

Unless a disposable aluminum pan really fits the occasion, your labor-of-love lasagna or Grandma's baked ziti is best assembled and baked in a heavy pan built for this kind of dish. Oven-safe glass, porcelain, or stainless steel can all handle the job, and don't have to be expensive. This pan is meant to be deeper, and ideally a bit longer and wider, than a nine-by-thirteen-inch pan. Get the largest pan that you have space for in your cabinets and in your oven, because if you're making lasagna or baked pasta, you might want to go big!

STAINLESS STEEL AND/OR ENAMELED CAST IRON COOKWARE AND DUTCH OVEN

Maybe you already have a few good pots and pans that serve you well. Maybe they're nonstick, and you love them, but you can't use them for high-heat cooking precisely because of that nonstick coating. Or maybe there are a few sizes of pots and pans you don't have and could really use. The best scenario is to have, in addition to nonstick gear, some stainless steel and/or enameled cast iron that can handle high heat when you want to sear meat or reduce a sauce. Choose options with metal handles so they're oven safe, too. Pick the sizes you think you'll use the most, and make sure to include a midsize Dutch oven for braised dishes like the gochujang braised pork tenderloin on page 106.

WINEGLASSES AND BAR GLASSES

If you have the space and the desire to add nice glassware to your kitchen setup, here's a bit of helpful guidance. But first, a caveat: sommeliers and mixologists may feel strongly about the unique glassware needs for every beverage. Most homes don't have the capacity to hold that many glasses, and even if they did, it may feel excessive. So consider having **as many wineglasses as you have dinner plates**. If you feel the need to double down and have that many for red as well as for white, and to double it again for beer and sparkling, all the power to you if you can find the space. If you're looking to streamline the numbers, however, there is a school of thought among sommeliers that a single, well-designed glass should be able to accommodate all your red and white wine needs. Radical, right? But space-constrained wine drinkers may want to subscribe!

The basic design elements you're aiming for are clear, thin glass, with a stem (or stemless if that's your thing), and a bowl that's larger at the bottom than at the top of the glass. As for champagne and sparkling wine, flutes are lovely (and narrow), and coupes are wide and can double as cocktail glasses.

Speaking of **cocktail glasses**, you could easily get obsessive about specific glasses for specific drinks. But really, short of **martinis** and **margaritas** being super appealing in their namesake glasses, nice-looking multipurpose glasses will get the job done. Get a set of **highball** glasses and a set of **rocks** glasses (or **double rocks**—they're just a little bigger than regular rocks glasses, not double the size), and if you still have room, add a set of martini glasses or coupes.

If you'd like to add to **beer glass options**, beyond the standard **pint glasses** you may already have, there are numerous shapes and sizes meant to enhance the pleasure of drinking specific beers. In the interest of space, here are a couple of options to start with, and you can certainly keep going from there:

Pilsner glass: They're nice for lighter beers like pale ales and lagers, German beer, and of course, pilsners.

Tulip glass: They look great and let some IPAs, stouts, and Belgian ales taste their best.

GEAR YOU DON'T REALLY NEED (AT LEAST FOR NOW)

If you already have a nonstick pan, and are adding stainless steel or enameled cast iron pans, you don't also need a regular cast iron skillet. Cast iron is fantastic, and if you're a fan, you can use it instead of, or in addition to, stainless steel or enameled iron. If you're new to cast iron, just be aware that you need to season it, or buy one that's preseasoned.

The highest end, top-of-the-line stainless steel (or copper, for that matter) pots and pans are unnecessary. The top brands typically have multiple cookware lines, and anything in the entry or midlevel range will set you up for life. If you're interested in professional-level pans, you're probably not reading this anyway.

You probably don't need a mortar and pestle. They're great looking, but chances are you'll reach for the blender or food processor first to save time.

Don't waste the money or the space on special egg poachers or omelet pans. A regular saucepan and/or skillet will do the same job.

In theory, a stovetop griddle is a great idea, but moving it on and off the stove, and finding a convenient spot to store it when it's not in use, might outweigh the joy of using it.

Register Now!

High-quality, long-lasting kitchen gear can be expensive, so if you're setting up a first-time kitchen with the power of a wedding registry behind you, you are very lucky. Besides whisks and wooden spoons and other reasonably priced items, include a few things that are on the pricier, will-last-forever end of the spectrum. They're great for group gifts and rich uncles. When you're first starting out, a registry is an opportunity to add nice gear to the kitchen that you'll use throughout your cooking and eating life, but that you aren't in a position to buy for yourself. Every time you stir a sauce in that amazing pan with your favorite wooden spoon, or turn on the stand mixer to make a cake in your beautiful Bundt pan, you'll think of all the lovely people who helped you set up your kitchen.

TOP TEN ITEMS TO REGISTER FOR

This stuff can be as expensive as it is awesome, and setting up a home *does* take a village, so I recommend adding these ten things to your wedding registry (provided you don't own any of them already), so the one-percenters and your grandma's Bridge club will know what to get you.

1. large and/or medium enameled cast iron Dutch oven

2. large stainless steel roasting pan

3. set of heavy stainless steel pots and pans with lids

4. stand mixer

5. top-of-the-line toaster or toaster oven

6. waffle maker

7. food processor

8. blender

9. knives: chef's knife, paring knife, steak knives

10. large heavy-duty wood cutting/carving board

EXPAND YOUR PANTRY

In addition to your established lineup of pantry basics (see the first section of this book) and confidence working with those ingredients, at some point you'll feel ready to stretch beyond that initial comfort zone. Maybe you're wondering whether you could actually cook some of the food that you like to eat when you're out at restaurants. Or you've noticed food magazines and cookbook covers featuring beautiful things you wish you could make. I'm here to tell you that all of it (okay, most of it; we can't control for all the variables) is within your reach. So here is a short list of additional ingredients for your culinary arsenal, based to some extent on restaurant cuisines and what's popular in the food world at the moment. The list is far from exhaustive, as possibilities for cuisine types are too numerous to list, but it is hoped it will get you thinking about the ingredients you'd like to incorporate into your repertoire.

- more salt options
- anchovies
- Worcestershire sauce
- jarred roasted red peppers
- additional vinegars
- toasted sesame oil
- hot sauces
- coconut milk
- Thai curry paste
- miso
- fish sauce
- Spanish paprika
- pumpkin pie spice
- turmeric powder
- cardamom
- coriander
- fennel seeds
- za'atar
- sumac
- tahini
- dried chilis
- chili powder

MORE SALT OPTIONS

There are so many interesting salts on the market, from flaked, specialized options like French fleur de sel, English Maldon salt, and Himalayan pink salt, and so many more, to options flavored with black truffle or smoked woods, just to name a few. A pinch of any of these can punch up the flavor of a dish and add a little crunch when sprinkled on food just before serving.

ANCHOVIES

Anchovies pack a ton of flavor in a tiny package. They melt into sauces, dressings (hail, Caesar!), and pasta dishes, and because they dissolve without a trace, you won't quite know they're there, except for the inexplicably wonderful depth of flavor they leave behind. An unopened tin will last a year in your pantry; opened and covered, leftover anchovies can be stored in the fridge up to two months. Anchovy paste is another good option, and is sold in tubes (like some tomato paste). Unopened, it can last up to eighteen months, stored in a cool dark place. Once open, it needs to be refrigerated, and can last up to a year in the fridge.

WORCESTERSHIRE SAUCE

Here's another great flavor bomb. Because of its savory brightness, a dash is a genius secret ingredient in cocktail sauce (and cocktails, too!), slow-cooked favorites like meaty (and nonmeaty) stews and soups, and in marinades as an interesting swap for vinegar, soy sauce, or even fish sauce. Together with a handful of other staples, Worcestershire and anchovies set the stage for a very nice Caesar dressing.

JARRED ROASTED
RED PEPPERS

Jarred roasted red peppers are also a solid addition to your pantry. They're nice on sandwiches, with scrambled eggs, in salads, and as a key ingredient in easy Greek yogurt– or sour cream–based dips, as well as romesco, the Spanish sauce/dip that also includes stale bread, garlic, almonds, and olive oil.

ADDITIONAL VINEGARS

Sherry vinegar has a deep, almost warm flavor that is great on salads, as a finishing touch in soups, including gazpacho, and a key flavor in romesco sauce. It has a more robust flavor than red wine vinegar without being sweet like balsamic vinegar.

Rice vinegar (also called rice wine vinegar) is considerably less acidic than wine or cider vinegar, and has a mild delicate flavor. It's great in slaws and for pickling. Seasoned rice vinegar is rice vinegar with added sugar (or corn syrup) and salt or MSG. Unless you have a specific reason for buying it, don't—regular rice vinegar is the better option.

TOASTED SESAME OIL

Oil from raw sesame seeds has a light color and relatively subtle flavor, but **toasted sesame oil** (also called dark sesame oil) is made from toasted sesame seeds, and has a rich, dark color and bold, nutty flavor. It's a key ingredient in many noodle and stir-fry dishes, and is often used in sauces, marinades, and as a finishing oil. Keep it in the refrigerator to extend its shelf life.

HOT SAUCES

Unless you have a strong aversion to anything spicy, a pantry for a more grown-up kitchen should always have some hot sauce in it. **Sriracha** is a red jalapeño-based sauce that's spicy, salty, vinegary, garlicky, and a little bit sweet. You can use this much-loved hot sauce straight up as a condiment on everything from scrambled eggs to burgers, or mix it into sauces, soups, or beans. There are lots of hot sauces out there, so if Sriracha's not your thing, find one you like. Another option, **gochujang**, is a thick Korean red chili paste that's super flavorful and spicy. A little added to marinades and dipping sauces, or at the end of cooking a soup or stew, goes a long way.

COCONUT MILK

Creamy, rich canned coconut milk is essential in many curries, soups, and marinades. Keep a can or two in the pantry, as it lasts at least a year and a half if not longer. On grocery store shelves, you may see cans of coconut milk and "lite" or reduced-fat coconut milk. Before reaching for the latter, know that it is a watered-down version of the full-fat variety, to which some thickeners may have been added. It could be a fine substitute in some cases, but not all. If a recipe calls for coconut milk, use the regular stuff for best results.

THAI CURRY PASTE

There are actually three versions of Thai curry paste: green, yellow, and red. Green is made with fresh chilis and is the spiciest of the three. Yellow includes some curry powder and some chilis, and is usually the mildest. Red, which is made with dried red chilis, is pretty hot, but not quite as intense as green. All three versions are built on a base that includes big flavors like garlic, lemongrass, and shrimp paste. Curry paste is a great way to add a blast of flavor to anything from stir-fries to steamed mussels.

MISO

Made from fermented soybeans, this Japanese staple is excellent added to sauces, glazes, and marinades. It's also a key ingredient in its namesake soup. Miso ranges in color from pale yellow to rich brown, and its flavors vary, too. Lighter options (known as white, yellow, or sweet miso) tend to be more delicate and sweeter, whereas darker miso (think red, brown, or barley), have a deeper, saltier flavor.

FISH SAUCE

Pungent, funky-tasting fish sauce is a recognizable flavor in pad Thai and green papaya salad, just to name a few dishes. It's made from fermenting anchovies, salt, and water, and delivers a big punch of flavor. A little goes a long way, but without it, those dishes just don't taste right.

SPANISH PAPRIKA

Also known as pimentón, or smoked paprika, this quintessential Spanish ingredient is made from peppers that are slowly dried over oak fires, which is what gives this spice its smoky flavor. It is available in three types—mild, medium, and spicy. A key flavor in chorizo, this spice is also essential in romesco sauce, and a pinch in deviled eggs makes them taste phenomenal. Smoked paprika can fill in for bacon if you don't have it, or are making a meatless dish and still want a smoky, savory element.

PUMPKIN PIE SPICE

Cinnamon on its own is often exactly what you need. But if your cooking calls for a combination of ground cinnamon, cloves, nutmeg, allspice, and ginger, **pumpkin pie spice** is the multitasker for you! Keep this flavor powerhouse in the pantry, and with one small jar you can do the job of five. (Add a sprinkle to coffee for a DIY pumpkin spice latte!) It's also nice in pancake and waffle batter, sauces, dips, desserts, on roasted butternut squash, and in savory dishes, too.

TURMERIC POWDER

This yellow-hued spice adds intense color and an under-tone of earthy flavor to everything from Indian curries to smoothies, along with stews and noodles.

CARDAMOM

Cardamom is a warm, aromatic, somewhat sweet spice used in many Indian, Middle Eastern, and Scandinavian dishes. It's a beloved ingredient in baked goods and savory dishes alike. If you're new to cardamom, know that a little goes a long way, and while you may see it sold in pods, ground cardamom is a fine place to start.

CORIANDER

Citrusy, warm, and a little sweet, coriander is the seed of the cilantro plant. It's popular in Indian, Middle Eastern, and some Asian cooking. It's a favorite in brining and pickling, and is a key ingredient in the Egyptian nut and spice blend called dukkah. You can buy coriander ground, and as seeds that you can grind yourself.

FENNEL SEEDS

Their slightly sweet, mild licorice flavor makes fennel seeds popular in cuisines from India to the Middle East to Europe. Their aroma and taste is recognizable in Italian sausage and Chai tea, just to name a few favorites.

ZA'ATAR

Za'atar is a Middle Eastern spice blend that's good on everything from pita to hummus to roasted vegetables. Actual recipes and proportions vary, but the list of ingredients usually includes ground dried oregano, thyme, ground sumac, toasted sesame seeds, and salt.

SUMAC

Sumac is a deep red berry that's dried and ground into a powder. It has a tart, sour, somewhat citrusy taste, and is popular in Middle Eastern and Mediterranean cooking. Sumac is often an ingredient in spice blends, marinades, and rubs, and is also nice sprinkled on food before serving.

TAHINI

Tahini is basically toasted ground sesame seeds. Its texture is like a thinner version of peanut butter. Besides chickpeas, tahini is the other main player in hummus. It's also delicious in dressings, baked goods (it could fit in just about anywhere you would use peanut butter), and as a dip for raw or cooked veggies.

DRIED CHILIS

Dried chili peppers of various kinds are used in pretty much all cuisines everywhere, from the American Southwest to Mexico, Europe, and Asia. From Mexican ancho, guajillo, chipotle, and chile de árbol to Italian pepperoncini to Szechuan dried red peppers, the list is very long. These dried peppers are often crushed and ground, or soaked and then ground with other ingredients to make sauces such as mole.

CHILI POWDER

Chili powder is a blend of dried chili peppers and other spices that's used in dishes such as chili con carne and dry rubs for grilling and barbecue. Because it is a blend of spices, there is no one singular chili powder; instead, the manufacturer decides on the proportions. And if you see **chile** powder in the spice aisle (notice that the word ends with an "e" rather than an "i"), that just means it's the ground version of the **chili** pepper that's named on the container.

Ways to Maximize Storage and Organization in Your More Grown-Up Kitchen

If you're lucky enough to be working with a huge kitchen that has all the space you need and all the organizational bells and whistles you want, good for you! But for most people who are working with a more grown-up kitchen that's not quite their forever home kitchen and may only be temporary, limited cabinet space and a lack of smart, plentiful, and built-in storage is likely the norm. To help with that, here are some game changers when it comes to maximizing storage and organization in your kitchen.

MAGNET BOARD FOR KNIVES

A magnetic knife rack is a great way to store knives safely and save counter space—see ya later clunky knife block! Mount one of these in a spot that's convenient, seems safe relative to the way you move around your kitchen, and above all, is inaccessible to children. Some favorite locations include: above the sink, behind the stove or on the backsplash, on the side of a cabinet, or to the side of the stove.

HANGING POT AND PAN RACK

Hanging pots and pans is a great way to save cabinet space and at the same time have everyday items within reach. A ceiling-mounted or wall-mounted rack can also be a nice design element in your kitchen.

PEGBOARD WITH HOOKS FOR POTS, PANS, AND UTENSILS

Shelves are great, but if you mount a large pegboard on your wall, you can hold even more gear. Once the pegboard is mounted, buy some S hooks and you'll be ready to hang pots, pans, and even canisters that hold utensils. Fun fact: Julia Child kept her kitchen organized with pegboard.

MUG HOOKS

Install small hooks to the underside of a cabinet shelf or the underside of the bottom of your cabinets to hang coffee cups. There will still be room for plates or saucers underneath the mugs if you install the hooks inside a cabinet, and you'll free up counter space if you install them under the cabinets. Plus, the whole thing looks adorable.

SHELVES ANYWHERE YOU CAN INSTALL THEM

Put up some glass shelves above the sink if you have cabinets on either side. Glass is nice because it won't warp if a little water splashes onto it, and if you have a window in front of your sink, a glass shelf will maximize your view! Installing shelving inside of tall cabinets will add extra storage and make it easier to move things around.

DIVIDERS IN CABINETS TO MAXIMIZE SPACE

Dividers serve a similar purpose in comparison to shelves, but they can be placed vertically inside cabinets. They're a good way to keep sheet pans, muffin tins, cooling racks, and trays standing up, organized, and easy to grab.

OVER-THE-SINK CUTTING BOARD TO MAXIMIZE WORK SPACE

When work space is tight in your more grown-up starter kitchen, this two-in-one idea is fantastically efficient—you gain counter space and a work surface for slicing, dicing, and chopping all in one. There are various versions of this item—from a solid board with a lip that fits over the edge of the counter to hold the board steady on top of the sink, to options with adjustable slide-out metal handles so the board will span the width of any size sink. Some models even offer a removable colander so you can rinse and drain food directly over the sink as you ready it for slicing and dicing.

USE THE INSIDES OF CABINET DOORS

The insides of cabinet doors are prime, untapped real estate. You can attach to them a holder for your **pot lids** or a dispenser for reusable grocery store **plastic** bags or large **kitchen trash bags**. They're great spots to mount a **spice rack**, to install a **bar of hooks** for hanging **utensils** or **pot holders**, or to have hooks for hanging cleaning **rags and gloves**. Another great use for this space to install **corkboards** and/or **chalkboards** on them in order to keep important notes handy.

SILICONE POT AND PAN DIVIDERS

When you have nonstick cookware, you don't want to stack other metal pots on top of them or you can end up scratching the surface of the nonstick ones, which is a bad thing because it means they won't work as well. Plus, small amounts of the nonstick coating could get into your food when you do cook with them. An easy and attractive way to avoid all of this is to keep silicone dividers in between pots and pans. Better still, these dividers are great to toss onto the table and use as trivets.

BASKETS AND BINS

Inside of drawers and cabinets, as well as on pantry shelves, bins and baskets are a great way to keep tools and food items organized. Choose clear or opaque, modern, or traditional.

TECHNIQUES AND PRIMERS

With slightly more grown-up digs and a little more space, you may feel the urge to invite more people over. I've got you covered. A beautiful cheese board is your ace in the hole. Include it with the guacamole (see page 48) and a crudité platter with the prettiest vegetables, and you're on your way to a having a party. Want to turn it into a dinner party? Add some of the recipes that follow, and you're there.

CHEESE BOARD

People love cheese boards, and they are nearly always happy to be greeted by one at a dinner or a party. There are no hard-and-fast rules when it comes to assembling them either. Experts often suggest offering a variety of cheeses, which can include the types of milk the cheeses are made from or the textures and flavors of the cheeses.

Have at least three or four different cheeses on the board, choose ones that you like, and don't be boring. And *always* set out a knife for each cheese, as well as a few accompaniments such as crackers, nuts, fruit, condiments, pickles, and veggies with the board.

One last thing: for optimal flavor, take the cheeses out of the fridge an hour before you plan to serve them.

CHEESE CATEGORIES:

- firm/aged (cheddar, Asiago, Manchego, Mimolette, Parmigiano-Reggiano, Grana Padano)

- semisoft (Gouda, fontina, Monterey Jack)

- soft and/or ripened (goat cheese, Stracchino, Taleggio, Brie, Camembert)

- blue (Gorgonzola, Stilton, Roquefort)

ACCOMPANIMENTS:

- crackers, bread sticks, and sliced bread

- nuts—favorites include almonds, Marcona almonds, pistachios, cashews, and walnuts; sweet-and-salty roasted (as well as sweet-salty-spicy roasted) nuts are also great

- jarred condiments like fig preserves, chutney, olives, and pickled vegetables

- seasonal fruits, including grapes, cherries, apples, pears, figs, and berries

HOW MUCH TO BUY?

If the cheese board is meant as an appetizer or is part of a bigger spread of foods at a party, anywhere between one and four ounces of each cheese per person is a good rule of thumb. And it's always better to have extra cheese rather than not enough.

BLANCHING VEGETABLES

If you've ever encountered a platter of vegetables and dip (maybe it's sitting next to that beautiful cheese board), picked up a raw broccoli floret, taken a bite, and wondered who likes broccoli like that, then you will be glad to learn about blanching.

It's a simple cooking technique that brings out vegetables' vibrant color and gently improves their texture and flavor. It's exactly what vegetables like broccoli, cauliflower, green beans, asparagus, and sugar snap peas need when you're putting them on a platter with dip or using them in a stir-fry.

Blanching works by submerging the raw vegetables in a pot of salted, boiling water for a minute or two, then lifting them out with a slotted spoon and plunging them into ice water, which stops the cooking process. That's it. They're done. Just drain and serve. You can also do this with fresh vegetables you plan to freeze—like if you buy too much at the farmers market and want to save it for another time. Simply blanch the vegetables, pat them dry, put them in a zip-top bag, and stash them in the freezer.

SAUTÉING

Sautéing, which is also sometimes referred to as pan frying, means to cook food, usually vegetables and thin cuts of meat, in a pan with a small amount of fat over relatively high heat. It gives food a browned, crispy exterior and a moist interior. One important trick to remember when sautéing is to *not* add too much food to the pan at once—this crowding will cause the food to steam rather than brown. Also, with meat especially, don't start trying to move or flip the food right away. Instead, let the food cook undisturbed until it can be moved without pulling or tearing. At this moment, it will be nicely browned and is ready to flip.

BASIC CHEESE SAUCE FOR MACARONI AND CHEESE

Once you've mastered this basic method, you can switch up the cheeses and use it for standard mac and cheese made with cheddar, as well as more elaborate baked pasta creations such as the antipasto platter pasta bake on page 108. The idea is that you're making a roux (a French culinary term for when you cook flour and fat so it can act as a thickener for sauces), stirring in warm milk, mixing it on the stovetop for a few minutes until it thickens, and then seasoning it and adding cheese.

Here's an easy-to-remember formula: melt 2 tablespoons **unsalted butter** in a saucepan on medium-low heat. Add 2 tablespoons of **flour** and whisk for 2 minutes. Slowly pour in 2 cups of warm **milk**. Stir for about 5 minutes until the mixture thickens. Season with **salt** and

pepper and turn off the heat. Stir in 1 1/2 cups of your favorite grated or shredded **cheese**, and that's it!

SMOOTHIE BOWL FORMULA

Why gulp down a smoothie through a straw when you can use a spoon to enjoy one in a bowl that you've topped with fruit, nuts, seeds, and everything else you like? Smoothie bowls feel like a meal. They're quick and easy to make, and the flavor and texture combinations are endless. Follow this basic formula and you're ready to blend.

Into your blender canister, add:

- 1 cup of frozen fruit plus a banana—this acts as the base

- 1/2 cup liquid such as milk (dairy or nondairy), yogurt, coconut water, or a fresh juice like carrot juice

- 1 tablespoon of nut butter and/or sweetener (add more or less to taste) for body and flavor

- Optional 1/2 cup leafy greens like kale or spinach (that you've cleaned, stemmed, and chopped)

- Optional scoop of protein powder

Blend on low until desired consistency is reached. Spoon into a bowl and top with sliced or chopped fruit or berries and a tablespoon each of your favorite nuts, seeds, granola, shredded coconut, or dry cereal for crunch.

RECIPES

With these recipes, you'll be dinner-party ready, or dinner-ready if there's no party. Pair the classic roasted chicken with the perfect mashed potatoes, or serve the gochujang braised pork tenderloin with steamed rice. The shaved Brussels sprouts or another fresh, crunchy vegetable will round out the menu. And when you get around to inviting over a big group of friends, the antipasto platter pasta bake is the dinner to make. It's full of creamy, meaty, salty, cheesy goodness, and when you slide that big pan out of the oven and onto the table, you'll make everyone's night. All of these recipes are a step above basic, and they make great use of a lot of the gear you have in this kitchen. Additionally, all of them will call on pantry and/or fridge staples and kitchen linens.

CLASSIC ROASTED CHICKEN

Makes: 4 to 6 servings　　　**Total time:** 75 minutes
Gear: roasting pan or lasagna pan, instant-read thermometer

Simple is sometimes best. Here's a pared-down, reliable way to roast a chicken perfectly every time. After you've finished the chicken, toss the bones into a zip-top bag and freeze them to use later when you're making chicken stock.

Ingredients:
One 3-to-4-pound chicken

1 tablespoon kosher salt

2 teaspoons freshly ground
black pepper

Small bunch of fresh herbs
of your choosing, including
any combination of parsley,
rosemary, thyme, or oregano

Directions:

Preheat the oven to 450°F. In a small dish, mix the salt and pepper. Rinse the chicken well, inside and out, remove the giblets, if included, and pat it completely dry (inside and out) with paper towels.

Set the chicken in a roasting pan (if you have a roasting rack, use it; no problem if you don't, the chicken will still turn out great). Generously sprinkle the salt and pepper mixture inside the cavity, and all over the outside of the bird, as well. Place the herbs inside the cavity.

Place the pan in the preheated oven. Roast for 15 minutes, then lower the oven temperature to 425°F. Let it roast undisturbed until the chicken reaches an internal temperature of 165°F when checked with an instant-read thermometer at the thickest part of the thigh, about 50 to 60 minutes. Remove from the oven, and let it rest for 15 minutes before carving and serving the bird.

GOCHUJANG BRAISED PORK TENDERLOIN

Makes: 4 to 6 servings   **Total time:** about 60 minutes
Gear: rasp grater, knife, cutting board, mixing bowls, measuring spoons and cups, Dutch oven, tongs, saucepan

Delicious and quick enough for weeknight cooking, but nice enough for a dinner party, this dish can be served with simple steamed white rice and baby arugula (or your favorite salad green) lightly dressed with olive oil, rice wine vinegar, salt, and pepper.

Ingredients:

1 small shallot, finely chopped

6 garlic cloves, grated

1 tablespoon grated ginger

1/4 cup gochujang

1/4 cup reduced-sodium soy sauce

3 tablespoons sugar

1 tablespoon rice vinegar

1 tablespoon toasted sesame oil

1 1/2 teaspoons freshly ground black pepper, divided

2 pork tenderloins (1 pound each)

Kosher salt

2 tablespoons vegetable oil

1 cup low-sodium chicken broth

5 thinly sliced scallions, divided

Directions:

Preheat oven to 350°F. In a medium bowl, combine shallot, garlic, ginger, gochujang, soy sauce, sugar, vinegar, sesame oil, and 1 teaspoon pepper; set sauce aside.

Season pork all over with salt and remaining 1/2 teaspoon pepper. Heat oil in a Dutch oven over medium heat until hot. Add pork and cook, turning occasionally, until lightly browned on all sides, about 8 minutes. Transfer pork to a plate.

Add sauce to Dutch oven and bring to a simmer. Cook for 3 minutes; add broth, bring to a boil, then turn off heat. Return pork to Dutch oven, partially cover pot, and place in oven. Simmer until pork is tender, 45 to 55 minutes, turning pork in sauce once during cooking. Add half of scallions to pot during last 5 minutes of cooking.

Remove pork from oven and let rest 5 minutes. Cut into 1/2-inch-thick slices. Drizzle with some of the sauce, and serve remaining sauce on the side. For a thicker sauce, simmer it in a small saucepan on the stovetop until it reduces to desired consistency. For a smooth sauce, strain before serving. Garnish with remaining scallions.

ANTIPASTO PLATTER PASTA BAKE

Makes: 6 to 8 servings as a main course
Total time: 45 minutes
Gear: food processor, knife, measuring cups and spoons, mixing bowls, whisk, wooden spoon, cutting board, saucepan, colander, baking pan

This baked pasta pulls together all the bold, tangy, meaty, cheesy wonderful flavors of the antipasto platter in a big, crowd-friendly main course. To make it for a really big group, double the recipe, and bake it in a giant lasagna pan.

Ingredients:

8 ounces provolone or Asiago cheese

4 ounces salami, spicy or not, up to you

16-ounce jar giardiniera vegetables, rinsed and drained

1 cup Peppadew peppers, drained

12 ounces casarecce pasta, or any short pasta shape

2 tablespoons unsalted butter

2 tablespoons all-purpose flour

2 cups milk, heated but not boiling

1/2 teaspoon salt

Freshly ground black pepper

1/2 cup shredded Italian cheese blend

Fresh chopped parsley and/or torn basil

Directions:

Using the shredding blade on your food processor, shred the provolone or Asiago cheese. Set the cheese aside. Shred the salami, and transfer it to a bowl. Switch to the S blade for chopping, and add the vegetables and peppers. Pulse to coarsely chop, and then add to the bowl with the salami. If you don't have a food processor, you can buy preshredded Italian cheese blend, and sliced salami that you can chop into smaller pieces with a chef's knife. You can also chop the vegetables by hand.

Preheat oven to 425°F. Boil pasta in salted water according to package instructions. Drain and set aside.

Melt butter in a deep saucepan or Dutch oven over medium heat. Add flour, and whisk for 2 minutes. Slowly pour in heated milk, whisking as you go. Stir until the mixture thickens, about 5 minutes. Stir in salt and pepper, turn off the heat, and add the shredded provolone or Asiago (or Italian cheese blend), and stir until it melts.

Add the cooked pasta to the cheese sauce, and toss to coat. Add the shredded vegetables and salami, and stir to incorporate. Pour the mixture into a 9-by-13-inch baking pan, and sprinkle shredded Italian cheese on top. Slide into preheated oven, and bake until cheese melts and turns golden, about 8 to 10 minutes. Remove from oven and cool 5 minutes. Sprinkle parsley or basil on top and serve.

PERFECT MASHED POTATOES

Makes: 8 to 10 servings   **Total time:** 30 minutes
Gear: vegetable peeler, measuring cups and spoons, knife, cutting board, saucepan, colander, potato masher or ricer, wooden spoon

Here's the perfect version of this go-to side dish. The key is adding the butter first and then the milk. If you don't love chives, leave them out.

Ingredients:
3 pounds Yukon gold potatoes, peeled, rinsed, and cut into quarters

1 tablespoon plus
1 teaspoon salt, divided

3/4 cup milk

6 tablespoons
unsalted butter, melted

Freshly ground black pepper

2 tablespoons chopped chives (optional)

Directions:

Place potatoes in a large saucepan, cover with cold water, and bring to a boil. Add 1 tablespoon salt, and reduce heat to a simmer. Cook potatoes until they're tender, and can be pierced with a knife, 8 to 10 minutes. Meanwhile, heat the milk until it's warm, but do not let it boil.

Drain the potatoes, return them to the pot, and warm them on low for about a minute to evaporate any residual moisture. Mash the potatoes with a masher or ricer, then stir in the butter to fully incorporate it. Slowly pour in the milk, stirring as you go, until you reach the desired consistency. Season with remaining teaspoon salt and pepper, or more to taste. Fold in chives, if using. Serve immediately. Can also be covered and reheated in a microwave.

SHAVED BRUSSELS SPROUTS WITH LEMON AND GRANA PADANO

Makes: 6 servings   **Total time:** 20 minutes
Gear: food processor or mandoline, knife, citrus press, measuring cups and spoons, mixing bowl, tongs

This salad adds bright, bold flavor and crunch to any meal. It's an especially nice addition to a lineup that's heavy on rich, cooked dishes, like for Thanksgiving. Grana Padano is an Italian cow's milk cheese that's similar to Parmigiano-Reggiano in flavor and texture, but a bit softer. It's also considerably softer on the wallet.

Ingredients:

12 ounces fresh Brussels sprouts, cleaned and trimmed

2 tablespoons fresh lemon juice

1/2 cup grated Grana Padano cheese (or Parmigiano-Reggiano)

1/2 teaspoon salt

1/2 teaspoon freshly ground pepper

1 tablespoon olive oil

2 tablespoons roasted almonds, roughly chopped

Directions:

Shred the Brussels sprouts using the shredding blade on your food processor. You can also do this with a mandoline or use a knife, both of which will work fine but require a bit more time and effort. You'll need about 4 cups.

Place shredded Brussels sprouts in a large bowl; add remaining ingredients and toss to combine. Adjust for salt, lemon, and cheese, if necessary, to achieve desired balance of flavors. Serve immediately.

PUMPKIN CHOCOLATE CHIP CAKE

Makes: 12 slices   **Total time:** About 75 minutes

Gear: loaf pan, measuring cups and spoons, mixing bowls, whisk, handheld or stand mixer, wooden spoon, rubber scraper, cooling rack

Children and adults go nuts for this loaf cake. Bring it to a get-together, give it as a holiday gift, or just keep at home for yourself. It freezes well, too.

Ingredients:

2 1/4 cups all-purpose flour

1 1/2 teaspoons baking powder

3/4 teaspoon baking soda

3/4 teaspoon salt

1 teaspoon ground cinnamon

1 teaspoon pumpkin pie spice

One 15-ounce can pumpkin puree

1/2 cup melted butter (or neutral-flavored oil, if preferred)

2 large eggs

1 1/2 cups granulated sugar, plus 1 tablespoon for finishing

1 cup chocolate chips

Directions:

Preheat oven to 350°F. Spray a standard-size loaf pan with nonstick spray.

In a medium bowl, whisk together flour, baking powder, baking soda, salt, cinnamon, and pumpkin pie spice.

In the bowl of a stand mixer, combine pumpkin, butter, eggs, and 1 1/2 cups sugar and blend until smooth. Stir in chocolate chips. Transfer batter to prepared pan and smooth the top. Sprinkle remaining tablespoon of sugar across the top of batter.

Bake until a knife inserted into the center of the cake comes out clean, about 60 minutes. Cool in the pan for 10 minutes, then remove from pan, and cool completely on a rack. Store at room temperature.

CHECKLIST FOR A
MORE GROWN-UP KITCHEN

Here's a handy checklist that you can mark up and tear out. It includes all of the must-have gear and pantry essentials for a more grown-up kitchen, so you can keep track of what you have and what you need. I hope this list will make shopping and planning easy.

GEAR

- dinnerware
- flatware
- glassware
- mugs
- chef's knife
- paring knife
- serrated knife
- cutting boards
- nonstick pans
- saucepan with lid
- large pot and stockpot with lids
- rimmed baking sheet
- cooling rack
- baking dishes
- large lightweight bowl
- mixing bowls
- measuring cups and spoons
- glass storage containers with lids

- utensil holder
- vegetable peeler
- box grater
- whisk
- wooden spoon
- spatula
- rubber scraper
- spring-loaded tongs
- ladle
- slotted spoon
- offset spatula
- pepper mill
- corkscrew and can opener
- meat thermometer
- salad spinner
- colander and handheld strainer
- muffin and cupcake tin
- coffee maker and kettle
- coffee grinder
- toaster and/or toaster oven
- kitchen linens
- handheld electric mixer
- blender and food processor
- kitchen shears
- handheld mandoline-style slicer
- potato masher or ricer
- rasp grater
- handheld citrus juicer
- cake and pie pans
- lasagna pan
- stainless steel and/or enameled cast iron cookware and Dutch oven
- wineglasses and bar glasses

PANTRY ITEMS

- olive oil
- neutral-flavored oil
- nonstick spray
- red or white wine vinegar
- distilled white vinegar
- canned and jarred essentials
- salt (table and kosher) and pepper (or pepper-corns for a pepper mill)
- dried herbs and spices
- short and long pasta
- rice
- quinoa or couscous
- coffee and tea
- nuts, nut butters, preserves, and sweeteners
- honey and/or agave syrup

- onion
- garlic
- all-purpose flour
- baking soda
- baking powder
- light brown sugar
- granulated sugar
- vanilla extract
- almond extract
- semisweet chocolate chips
- cocoa powder
- oats
- parchment paper
- condiments
- avocados
- lemons and limes
- ginger
- eggs

- plain yogurt
- butter and
  cream cheese
- frozen necessities
- more salt options
- anchovies
- Worcestershire sauce
- jarred roasted
  red peppers
- additional vinegars
- hot sauces
- coconut milk
- Thai curry paste
- miso

- fish sauce
- Spanish paprika
- pumpkin pie spice
- turmeric powder
- cardamom
- coriander
- fennel seeds
- za'atar
- sumac
- tahini
- dried chilis
- chili powder

PART 3

FOR A LARGE OR FOREVER HOME KITCHEN

If you're reading this section, then your kitchen is large or likely in what you consider to be your "forever home" or "home for the foreseeable future." So settle in, spread out, and set up this kitchen with the plan that you're going to stay awhile. Now is the time to invest in well-organized drawers and cabinets. Install those pull-out shelves and racks so pots, pans, prepware, cookware, and serveware—like platters and serving utensils—can stay organized in the cabinets. Carve out space for a pantry, and set it up so everything's easy to find, reach, and use. Hopefully there's room to unpack (maybe even *display*!) special dishes and big, beautiful serving pieces that you've collected over the years. As for gear, we'll talk about some of the bells and whistles, and which matter most in this kitchen. And if it's your turn to host Thanksgiving, the primer on page 151 will help get you up and running for the big day—you've totally got this!

If you have kids, you might already (or will soon) be sharing your kitchen with them. Having more space and resources means there are plenty of ways to make this kitchen work for adults and kids, whether the kids are yours or are just visiting, and this section will walk you through it. It will also give you the skinny on expanding your pantry to include all the gear involved in the amazing baking recipes included at the end.

MORE GEAR TO CONSIDER

In addition to the gear listed in sections 1 and 2 on pages 3 and 71, you'd do well to consider including the following in your forever home starter kitchen, space and funds permitting. There are items that may have been on your wish list for a while, like a gorgeous stand mixer you've never had room for in other kitchens, let alone been willing to splurge on. Or a great-looking glass cake stand that would've taken up half the counter space in your previous kitchens. This more spacious kitchen presents an opportunity to expand your cooking repertoire with new tools and projects. This section will help you choose wisely so you have a warm, inviting space filled with gear that inspires you to cook.

- stand mixer
- countertop oven or fancy toaster
- wok
- more sheet pans of different sizes
- seven- or nine-quart enameled round iron Dutch oven
- extra-large, heavy-duty roasting pan
- gravy boat
- waffle maker
- mini muffin tins
- standing citrus press
- immersion blender
- air fryer
- multicooker
- spiralizer
- serving platters, bowls, and utensils
- rolling pin
- cake plate or cake stand

STAND MIXER

Even if you have a handheld electric mixer, it's really no stand-in for a stand mixer, which frees up your hands to do other things while it does the beating and whipping. If you have the counter space, leave this beauty out to be admired. It's great looking, and also happens to be incredibly heavy, so it's no fun to drag out from a cabinet every time you use it. At some point, consider buying an extra bowl and an extra paddle attachment so if you're making something like a layer cake, you can move between batter and frosting without stopping and washing everything in the middle.

Some brands also sell attachments for pasta making, vegetable spiralizing, and even sausage making, which can be enticing when you're delving deeper into advanced cooking and have more space.

COUNTERTOP OVEN OR FANCY TOASTER

If you don't already have a toaster or toaster oven that you *love*, a high-quality **countertop oven** can be a great thing to own. They're pricey for sure, like in the hundreds, but they can do a lot. Some models offer a convection feature, making an appliance known for its efficiency even quicker and more efficient at roasting a chicken, cooking some pork chops, and baking a nine-by-nine-inch pan of brownies. Plus, they can still warm up leftover pizza exceptionally well and toast a nice bagel. A fancy, retro-style toaster will set you back a similar amount. People love these appliances because in addition to their functionality, they're like kitchen jewelry—something beautiful you enjoy looking at when you use it every day.

WOK

A wok is an amazing piece of cookware you can use to stir-fry, steam, boil, and deep-fry, to name a few of its handy uses. In addition to a classic stir-fry like Grace Young's stir-fried spicy chicken and peppers on page 158, you can also use a wok to make french fries, mussels steamed with white wine and garlic, and even a big batch of popcorn. If you've held back from owning one because woks are large and you didn't have the space for it, hopefully now your kitchen can accommodate one. A flat-bottomed, carbon steel wok is the best, and ironically it's often the least expensive option, too. Don't be swayed by nonstick finishes or more expensive materials; carbon steel works best. After you season and start cooking in a carbon steel wok, it begins to develop a patina that will naturally become a nonstick finish. And the more you cook with it, the deeper this patina becomes. For everything you need to know about choosing, using, and caring for a wok, stir-fry guru Grace Young is the absolute authority: graceyoung.com.

MORE SHEET PANS OF DIFFERENT SIZES

Rimmed baking sheets are the cookware workhorses of the kitchen. The standard size, which is also called a half sheet, is well suited to tasks ranging from roasting vegetables and cut–up chicken to baking cookies and making kale chips. So what could possibly be better than having two half-sheet pans? Having more sheet pans! Add a quarter sheet to your collection (great for smaller jobs like toasting nuts and baking a few potatoes) as well as an extra-large (three-quarter) sheet, a size that might take up a full rack in your oven (be sure to measure your oven before buying). The extra-large sheet pan is a lifesaver for those times when you need a little more space than a standard half sheet provides in order to fit all your vegetables in a single layer without crowding. By adding both of these to your lineup, you will be prepared for all sheet-pan situations.

SEVEN- OR NINE-QUART ENAMELED ROUND IRON DUTCH OVEN

Big, heavy, and built to last, this huge Dutch oven is the kitchen equivalent of a 1980s Volvo station wagon. Keep this pot someplace you can easily hoist it onto the stovetop, because it weighs a ton even without food in it. But the beauty of this kind of pot (in addition to some manufacturers selling it with a lifetime guarantee) is the exquisite way it conducts heat, distributing it evenly so food cooks perfectly, and its smooth interior that helps prevent food from sticking. This item is exactly what you want for braised short ribs; a big, long-simmering pot of ragu; or a triple batch of perfect tomato sauce.

EXTRA-LARGE, HEAVY-DUTY ROASTING PAN

Thanksgiving turkey, giant lasagna, pork butt roast—these are just a few reasons you'd want a hulking roasting pan. While you might be able to make some of those things in a Dutch oven, a roasting pan is more shallow and allows air to circulate around the food. It's the pan to use when you want browning. Heavy stainless steel is ideal, and it's also wise to buy the largest one that will fit in your oven (measure carefully before you buy, and be sure to account for the space the handles take up). If you ever want to use it for gravy (and if you make a turkey in it, you surely will), don't get a nonstick pan. You don't want to worry about scraping the nonstick finish or having constraints on how high you can turn up the heat. If you're going to use this to roast meat or a turkey (read more about Thanksgiving on page 151), you'll use a roasting rack set into the pan. This helps lift the food so the hot air can circulate around it. The rack is a separate item from the pan. Sometimes they're sold together as a set, but racks are inexpensive and can also be purchased separately.

GRAVY BOAT

Without one of these (it's nice to have more than one if you host big dinners and holidays), your only option is to serve that lovely béarnaise sauce you just slaved over or your gorgeous Thanksgiving turkey gravy from a measuring cup, and that's just unsightly. A gravy boat, which is not expensive and admittedly may not get used frequently, needs to be ready and waiting when you need it.

WAFFLE MAKER

Here's a piece of gear that you absolutely *don't* need until the moment that you do. And that moment, when you feel you *must* make waffles, will inevitably arise on a lazy weekend morning, when the last thing you want to do is go out and buy a waffle maker. So think preemptively on this one. It's a good gadget to have on hand, and a nice one will last a very long time. There are two basic types of waffles: thick, fluffy ones with deep pockets (sometimes called Belgian style), or thinner, crispier waffles with shallow pockets (American style). Choose the style you like, and then buy a waffle maker that makes that type. Almost all waffle makers are nonstick, and relatively easy to clean. For a brunch party, set up a waffle maker and a batch of batter (on ice) next to it, and let guests have a do-it-yourself waffle moment. It'll be fun with the bagels, fruit salad, and frittata that you're probably serving as well.

MINI MUFFIN TINS

Sometimes less is more. These muffin tins are for those times when you'd be happy to eat (or for your kids to eat) just a little bit of something sweet rather than the full-size version. While you may not use it as often as its full-size counterpart, it's a great, inexpensive addition to your bakeware lineup if you have the space.

STANDING CITRUS PRESS

You may already have a handheld juice press. It can fit in a drawer and is relatively inexpensive and incredibly useful. Equally useful, and definitely the best when you need more than a few ounces of juice, is the standing citrus press, a retro-style statement piece that looks fantastic on any kitchen countertop or bar. Kids will have a blast pulling down the lever on lemons to help make a pitcher of lemonade, and adults will appreciate the stylish design, fresh-squeezed juice, and the possibilities for making cocktails. There are also many electric versions of this tool.

IMMERSION BLENDER

This smallish, not-too-expensive, easy-to-use gadget is incredibly convenient for pureeing soup directly in the pot.

Basically it's an electric wand that you can hold in one hand (presumably while holding a pot handle in the other) and immerse into a pot of soup or applesauce. In less than a minute you'll transform cooked vegetables or fruit into a silky puree. Some models even make whipped cream!

AIR FRYER

This moderately priced appliance is having a moment. If you have the space for one (most are about the size of a toaster oven), read on. Basically, an air fryer uses a little bit of oil and a lot of hot, circulating air to cook food so it has a nice, crispy outer layer. Similar to a convection oven, it does a good job with everything from french fries and roasted vegetables to chicken and perfectly reheated foods from the fridge or freezer, as long as these foods are in small batches. While it's hard to make a case that anyone truly *needs* an air fryer, it's also true that this piece of gear can do its crispy good work in less time, and often with tastier results, than a full-size oven or a toaster oven.

MULTICOOKER

Who knows how long the craze for this gadget will go on. Maybe it's here to stay. People who love it swear by its magical ability to turn pots of beans and big hunks of meat exquisitely tender and deliciously flavorful in a fraction of the time it would take on the stovetop or in the oven. And there's no denying the allure of a gadget that's an electric pressure cooker, a slow cooker, a rice cooker, and yogurt maker all in one. Even just calculating how much counter space it could save is enough to make a space-challenged newbie cook swoon. But some people remain unimpressed, and feel its strengths are limited and footprint too big. If you're on the fence, see if you can borrow a friend's for a test drive.

SPIRALIZER

Perhaps you've seen zucchini noodles (or their siblings made from squash, beets, sweet potatoes, or carrots) in the produce section at the grocery store. They're an interesting way to eat more vegetables and use less higher-carb pasta in dishes that are traditionally pasta-based. If you like vegetable noodles and want to eat them a lot, a spiralizer is an inexpensive gadget you can use to make them at home. This is one of those tools that's loved by some (the ones who use it all the time), and not by others (possibly the ones who dread cleaning it). There are small, handheld spiralizers that work sort of like pencil sharpeners, as well as countertop models, and spiralizing attachments for standing mixers as well. There are even electric ones if you're totally committed to eating veggie noodles.

SERVING PLATTERS, BOWLS, AND UTENSILS

It's incredible how much the right presentation can add to, or take away from, a dish. The same way that a great outfit can make you feel like a million bucks for a special event, that gorgeous shaved salad you carefully prepare needs to show up on the table in the right platter or bowl that lets its colors pop and holds its quantity just right; not too big or too small. Food should look as fantastic as it tastes. White serving platters and bowls are always reliable for making most food look great. You need a variety of shapes—oval, round, and rectangular—in various sizes, some shallow and some deeper, some with edges and some without. And be sure to buy attractive serving forks and spoons to go along with all of these platters and bowls.

Tip: One way to display your cool collection of platters is to mount them on the wall. You can choose a mounting option where the platters would still be accessible and usable, or if they're more for show, consider framing them all in clear acrylic boxes and then lining those frames up to fill a wall. Another, more user-friendly way to simultaneously store and display platters is to build a large plate rack onto the end of a row of cabinets.

CAKE PLATE OR CAKE STAND

Cake plates and stands allow you to put your beautiful baked goods on a pedestal. Literally. Stands and plates also make it easier for you to cut and serve the baked goods. Some come with an elegant, domed glass cover, which is called a cloche (yep, same name as the cute 1920s hat).

KIDS IN THE KITCHEN

Being in a forever home might mean sharing the kitchen with kids, and all the things they like to make and eat. Whether the kids are yours or your nieces and nephews, grandkids, family friends, or neighbors, below you'll find a collection of cooking and eating ideas to keep things fun, tidy, practical, engaging, and delicious. You'll also find a special baking section that pulls together the pantry essentials you should keep on hand for baking projects with and for kids. Honestly, everything in this section is also for adults, especially around birthdays, parties, and holidays. Think of it as festive baking! Whether or not you have kids on the scene, making room in the pantry for things like cupcake liners and sprinkles can only have a positive effect on the overall mood of your kitchen.

DINING IN STYLE WITH KIDS

It's great to have a few sets of cups and dishes on hand that are just for kids. The portions are scaled to them, and the materials are not breakable. If you prefer to avoid plastic, a nice set in stainless steel or enamelware will last forever. For the littlest ones in high chairs or even new eaters at the table, easy-to-care-for (or even disposable) place mats and floor mats will save tabletops and floors, and the nice rug you may have under the dining table.

COOKING GEAR FOR LITTLE HELPERS

Many kids like to help with the cooking—and it's something they can start doing (a little bit) as soon as they're old enough to hold a bowl and a spoon. I don't mean to imply that preschoolers can help get dinner on the table, but if helping in the kitchen seems fun when they're little, they may stay interested. And one of the benefits is that kids who help prepare foods can be more open to tasting and eating them. Start by keeping a few plastic bowls and some kids-only mixing spoons and spatulas on hand for the littlest ones, and consider a more advanced set (with kid-friendly knives, utensils, prep, and baking tools) for enthusiastic older little cooks.

1. SMALL APRONS

Kids like wearing aprons, and they really do save their clothes from total ruin. So yes, have a few on hand.

2. STEP STOOLS

When kid cooks want to be up where the action is, they need one of these. If you have multiple wee ones helping in the kitchen, naturally each will insist on having their own small riser. You'll also use it yourself to reach to those cabinets above the fridge where you can barely see anything even *with* a step stool.

BAKING WITH KIDS

1. SPRINKLES

This is more a category than an item. There are so many shapes and types, and so many variations in size and color. Some of the most recognizable are jimmies, dragées, nonpareils, and colored sugars such as sanding sugar and coarse sugar. These are always a hit, and great to keep on hand in various color themes.

2. CAKE TESTERS

Toothpicks might be fine sometimes, but when you need something longer, consider a skewer, a thin knife, or an actual cake tester, which is essentially a sturdy, thin wire with a grip handle at the end.

3. CUPCAKE LINERS

Cupcake liners are always a kid favorite for holidays and occasions. It's also handy to keep some colorful, nonholiday ones in the pantry, too.

4. FOOD COLORING

Gotta have it! The more, the better. There are color sets out there from super basic to neon to professional level.

5. POWDERED SUGAR

A pantry must for all your icing and frosting needs, and for dusting on simple cakes.

6. ROLLING PIN

You'll use one of these to roll out cookie dough and make pie crust, and for more advanced pastry and baking projects, if you choose. There are numerous styles and materials to pick from, and even though the classic American rolling pin with handles may seem like the obvious choice it isn't necessarily the best. In fact, a tapered French-style rolling pin or a straight-sided dowel-style pin made of wood (without handles) are both longer, narrower, and easier to work with than the shorter, thicker, more iconic American model.

7. COOKIE CUTTERS

Seasonal cookie cutters are great, along with the more evergreen ones like animals, letters, and shapes.

8. DECORATING TOOLS—FROSTING IN TUBES, TIPS FOR THE TUBES, STENCILS

Decorating cookies and cupcakes using colored frostings and gels in tubes with cool tips is basically edible arts and crafts for kids, and they love it. Keep a bunch of colors and tip shapes on hand. Stencils can be great fun to use on full-size cakes. Set them on (or hold them over) a cake and dust with powdered sugar or cocoa powder. Remove the stencil and voilà!

9. GLUTEN-FREE FLOUR

Even if your family is fine with gluten, eventually a friend of your child's—or yours—with an allergy or intolerance will be in your home, and this is an easy way to make sure they're included.

10. COCONUT OIL

It's useful to have a nondairy oil that also adds flavor. In some recipes, you can swap out butter for coconut oil and have a delicious vegan variation.

11. CAKE MIXES AND HOMEMADE FROSTING

A friend with daughters the same ages as mine, who is an excellent cook and recipe developer, told me this trick when our kids were little: a boxed cake mix makes nice, fluffy cupcakes for a kids' party. Make your own frosting and you end up with amazing cupcakes. Genius. Keep a few boxes of vanilla and chocolate cake mix in the pantry and you're ready for anything.

TRANSPORTING BAKED GOODS

Between birthdays and parties and school events, it's a sure bet that at some point you will schlep batches of frosted sweets from your kitchen to another location. When that time comes, a sturdy carrier, or two, for cookies, cakes, and cupcakes is essential for moving the goods and keeping their beauty and integrity intact. These carriers come in various shapes and sizes, and are usually multilevel affairs with grooves or holders inside to keep items from tumbling around. They are typically round or rectangular, and some come with an option for carrying a full-size round or rectangular cake. Choose one that can go in the dishwasher.

GEAR YOU PROBABLY STILL DON'T NEED

- A panini press, if that's even still a thing.

- Tagines and paella pans, unless of course you're committed to cooking tagines and paella, then by all means.

- A soufflé pan. Until you decide to start making soufflés regularly, you don't need this.

- A trifle bowl. It's a beautiful glass bowl, for sure, sitting on its pedestal the way it does, but in a pinch you can use a regular glass bowl, and then go buy a trifle bowl for next time, which you may decide is never happening again.

- A fondue set. Unless the seventies come storming back, forget it. You'll use this once. Maybe twice.

- Canning gear. The impulse to can is fabulous. But the reality is that it takes time and planning, and somewhere in there is when you buy all that canning gear. No reason to have it taking up space any sooner than you need it to.

TECHNIQUES AND PRIMERS

Now that you have room for bigger cooking projects, you may as well take on some of the most rewarding ones first. A giant pot of chicken (or beef or vegetable) stock or broth pays back your efforts in dividends. Put a big stockpot on the stove and spend an afternoon simmering, straining, cooling, portioning, and freezing the results. You'll have a stash of liquid gold for next-level soups, stews, gravies, and pan sauces. On a less grand scale but just as beloved, homemade frosting makes every cake taste fantastic, so pull out your standing mixer and let it rip! Finally, you'll find a primer on Thanksgiving basic training. This could be your year to do it. You've got the kitchen, so start savoring all the fun you'll have planning, prepping, and pulling off the Olympics of cooking events.

MAKING STOCK AND BROTH

Stock and broth are actually different things. In terms of use, they can be interchangeable, but it's good to know how they differ, and then make what you prefer. Stock relies more heavily on bones than broth does, and sometimes the bones are roasted before going into the stockpot to maximize flavor. Bones give stock body thanks to the gelatin they release while cooking. Also, stock is not salted, whereas broth is. To make **stock**, you'll need bones, onions, carrots, celery, some peppercorns, parsley stems, and a bay leaf or two, and a large stockpot (at least 8 quarts; larger is preferred). After your stock simmers for four to six hours, you'll strain out the solids, cool it, and store in the fridge for three to four days or in the freezer for six months, and you can use it to make soups, sauces, and gravies.

To make **broth**, you'll need to add some meat and possibly some bones (for a pot of chicken broth, a few pounds of wings and necks offer a good combination of meat and bone), to a stockpot large enough to also hold a few coarsely chopped carrots, celery ribs, and an onion, 10 peppercorns, a bunch of parsley stems, a bay leaf or two, and enough water to cover everything by at least 2 inches. Simmer the broth anywhere from forty-five minutes to two hours. Strain out the solids, season with salt and pepper, and it's ready to use on its own or to make a quick soup, a stew, and even in place of water when making rice. Store broth in the refrigerator for four to five days, or in the freezer for up to six months.

Tip: A large pot of hot stock or broth will take a long time to cool on its own. One way to speed up

*the process, so you can transfer the liquid to stor-
age containers and refrigerate it, is to fill the sink
with ice and cold water, and set the pot into the
sink. Replenish the ice and water as needed until
the broth has cooled down.*

CAULIFLOWER RICE

Although it may sound odd or challenging, it's actually
pretty simple to turn a head of cauliflower into cauliflower
rice. The finished product can be eaten raw (like grains
added to a salad or tabbouleh), or cooked, where it's a close
equivalent to rice or couscous.

Here's how to make it: cut the head into quarters, and
cut out any tough parts of the inner core from each quarter.
Break the quarters into florets, and transfer them to the
food processor, in batches, if necessary—you only want to
fill the food processor about three-fourths of the way for
best results. Pulse in one-second intervals until the cauliflower is broken down into small granules. You can also
grate the cauliflower on a box grater for similar results.

For the cooked version, add raw "riced" cauliflower
and a tablespoon or two of butter or oil to a skillet and
cook on medium heat for about 5 minutes.

BUTTERCREAM FROSTING, ICING/GLAZING, AND WHIPPED CREAM

There are lots of options for topping and decorating cakes,
cookies, and desserts. A few of my favorite easy ones are

buttercream frosting, icing (meaning glazing and royal icing), and whipped cream. **Buttercream frosting** is basically softened unsalted butter that you beat vigorously or whip, and then add to it powdered sugar and flavor such as vanilla (or lemon, or chocolate, or matcha [powdered green tea], or whatever you like).

An easy buttercream recipe is: whip one cup of butter, gradually add three and one-half to four cups powdered sugar, and mix in one teaspoon of vanilla extract. If the frosting is too thick, add a tablespoon of milk or cream.

Icing (aka glaze) is a combination of powdered sugar and a bit of liquid that sets up quickly, and gets firmer as it dries.

A basic icing or glaze recipe is one cup powdered sugar mixed with one tablespoon milk and one tablespoon fresh lemon juice or one teaspoon vanilla extract.

Royal icing hardens to a candylike shell, and is made from powdered sugar, meringue powder or pasteurized egg whites (to avoid food safety concerns caused by bacteria such as salmonella that can be found in raw eggs), and flavorings like vanilla or lemon. It's typically used to decorate sugar cookies and gingerbread houses.

A basic formula is four cups of powdered sugar, one-fourth cup meringue powder, six tablespoons water, and one teaspoon vanilla extract or fresh lemon juice. You can substitute three pasteurized egg whites for the meringue powder and water.

Whipped cream is the perfect topping for pie, cake, and ice cream. The homemade version is simple to make, only takes a few minutes, and tastes amazing. Start by pouring a cold pint of heavy whipping cream into a large mixing bowl or the bowl of your stand mixer, and add a tablespoon or two of powdered sugar and a teaspoon of vanilla extract. Whip the cream with the handheld mixer or stand mixer on medium high (or by hand with a whisk). Whip the cream for a minute or two and stay close by, because it really goes quickly with an electric mixer. Whip until you see medium peaks forming: when you lift the beaters or whisk from the bowl, a slightly sturdy peak should form and gently hold. And that's it.

Hosting Thanksgiving

Depending on how many people you're inviting and the scope of your menu, cooking Thanksgiving dinner can be anything from a somewhat big deal to an event not unlike preparing for a marathon. The challenge boils down to this: you're not just prepping and cooking a lot of delicious food, you're also serving it, using a lot of bowls and platters, all at the same time and at the right temperature. If this is not your scene, don't even go there. Have a potluck or a Friendsgiving. But if you do like to cook, Thanksgiving dinner is a super fun challenge, and unless you *insist* on doing it all yourself, chances are you will have guests who are eager to help. One key piece of advice is to start thinking and planning in October.

Seriously. That's when you need to get a handle on the menu, gather recipes, find out how many people are coming, and begin making the many lists that will be the backbone of this project and keep it running like a Swiss watch.

In early November, assess your cookware, serveware, and flatware situation to know if there's anything you'll need to borrow or buy. Think about seating and table space. This is also the right time to begin shopping for paper goods, drinks, and recipe nonperishables. And if you're planning to make a turkey stock (it's fantastic for basting the turkey and making gravy), now's the time to make it and stash it in the freezer. Also, order your turkey now, too. Not sure how big a bird to buy? Calculate about one pound per person. If you love leftovers, bump it to a little more. Also consider two smaller turkeys for a big crowd rather than trying to fit one monster bird in the oven. And if a lot of guests like breast meat, roasting a separate turkey breast alongside a whole bird can solve that and allow you to buy a slightly smaller turkey.

Make lists of what can be prepped the week before the big day. The night before Thanksgiving, set the table and take out all the serving bowls and trays and utensils that you'll need (and put a note on each one to remind you what's going in it; when food is ready to hit the table, you don't want to be rethinking all of this). Make a list of every dish you're serving and tape it to a cabinet so you don't accidentally leave anything in the oven or the fridge, which almost always happens. And if you have kids who like crafts projects, ask them to make menus so your guests will know what's coming, and you'll have a memory of the day long after the leftovers are eaten and the kids are grown up.

RECIPES

Rather than choosing recipes based on whether or not you have the gear to make them, in this forever home kitchen you can make space for the gear you need to make all the recipes you want! Amazing lemon pistachio waffles may not be an everyday thing, but the waffle maker's in the cabinet, so that brunch is yours when you want it. Same goes for getting the urge to stir-fry chicken and vegetables on a weeknight in your big wok, or making a batch of crowd-pleasing mini muffins. You'll think nothing of reaching for a huge pot to make a double batch of escarole soup, or busting out your springform pan for a glorious almost flourless chocolate almond cake. In addition to the specific gear mentioned for each recipe, all of these will use pantry and/or fridge staples and kitchen linens.

LEMON PISTACHIO WAFFLES

Makes: 4 to 6 waffles   **Total time:** 25 minutes
Gear: measuring cups and spoons, rasp grater, citrus juicer, whisk, mixing bowls, wooden spoon, waffle maker, rimmed baking sheet with rack

This beautiful flavor combo of lemon and pistachio and buttery waffle tastes exceptional with a dusting of powdered sugar on top. But have no fear, maple syrup fans, your favorite also tastes great with these waffles.

Ingredients:

1 1/2 cups unbleached flour

6 tablespoons granulated sugar

2 teaspoons baking soda

1/2 teaspoon salt

2 eggs

1 cup milk

1 teaspoon vanilla extract

2 tablespoons fresh lemon juice

1 tablespoon lemon zest

6 tablespoons unsalted butter, melted

1 cup plain regular (not Greek) yogurt

1/4 cup chopped pistachios

Powdered sugar or maple syrup for serving

Directions:

In a medium bowl, combine flour, sugar, baking soda, and salt. In another bowl, whisk together eggs, milk, and vanilla until blended. Add this mixture to the dry ingredients and stir to combine. Stir in lemon juice and zest, then add melted butter and yogurt, stirring with a wooden spoon to combine. Let batter rest.

Preheat oven to warm (200°F), and turn on waffle maker, allowing it to heat up. When hot, pour 1/2 cup of batter onto the waffle maker and allow it to spread for a few seconds, then sprinkle 1 to 2 teaspoons chopped pistachios on top of batter. Close lid and wait for light to indicate that the waffle is ready. Open lid, remove baked waffle, and set it on a rack placed on a rimmed baking sheet to keep warm in the oven while you continue making waffles with remaining batter, adding finished waffles to pan in oven as you go. Serve topped with a dusting of powdered sugar or a drizzle of maple syrup.

GRACE YOUNG'S STIR-FRIED SPICY CHICKEN WITH PEPPERS

Makes: 3 servings with rice, or 4 servings as part of a multicourse meal

Total time: 20 minutes

Gear: knife, cutting board, measuring cups and spoons, mixing bowls, wok, spatula

As I mentioned in the section on woks on page 129, Grace Young knows a thing or two about stir-frying. She's pretty much the multiplatinum-award-winning authority on the subject. Her books on wok cookery are inspirational and indispensable, and her recipes are perfection. I am thrilled that she's sharing this recipe. It's easy to make, tastes fantastic, and is a great introduction to the wonders of the wok and stir-frying.

Ingredients:

1 pound boneless, skinless chicken breasts or thighs, cut into 1/4-inch-thick bite-size pieces

2 tablespoons dry sherry, divided

4 teaspoons soy sauce, divided

1 tablespoon minced ginger

2 teaspoons cornstarch

1 teaspoon plus 2 tablespoons peanut or vegetable oil, divided

3 tablespoons chicken broth

1 to 2 tablespoons Sriracha

1 tablespoon ketchup

1 tablespoon red miso

3 cloves garlic, smashed, peel removed

Ingredients (cont'd):

2 medium bell peppers, cut into 3/4-inch cubes, about 2 cups

2 scallions, trimmed and cut into 2-inch pieces

1/2 teaspoon salt

1/4 teaspoon sugar

Note: For a milder stir-fry use 1 tablespoon Sriracha. Use a mixture of red, green, yellow, and orange bell peppers for this stir-fry. Not all ketchups are the same. I prefer using Heinz.

Directions:

In a medium bowl, combine chicken, 1 tablespoon sherry, 2 teaspoons soy sauce, ginger, and cornstarch. Stir until cornstarch is no longer visible. Stir in 1 teaspoon oil. In a small bowl, combine broth, Sriracha, ketchup, miso, remaining 1 tablespoon sherry, and 2 teaspoons soy sauce. Stir until miso is dissolved.

Heat a 14-inch flat-bottomed wok or 12-inch skillet over high heat until a drop of water evaporates within 1 to 2 seconds of contact. Swirl in 1 tablespoon oil. Add the chicken and spread evenly in one layer in wok. Cook undisturbed 1 minute, letting chicken begin to sear. Stir-fry chicken 1 minute until it is no longer pink but not cooked through.

Swirl in remaining 1 tablespoon oil, add garlic, bell peppers, scallions, salt, and sugar, and stir-fry 1 minute or until just combined with chicken. Swirl sauce into wok and stir-fry 1 to 2 minutes or until chicken is cooked through and peppers are tender crisp.

ESCAROLE SOUP

Makes: 6 to 8 servings   **Total time:** 55 minutes
Gear: knife, cutting board, measuring cups and spoons, large pot, wooden spoon, salad spinner, citrus juicer

This soup is warm and cozy, easy to make, and delicious. Of course you'll use some of the homemade stock you have tucked away in the freezer. Consider doubling the recipe and making it in your biggest pot or Dutch oven. It's that good, and it freezes beautifully.

Ingredients:
2 tablespoons butter

1/2 cup chopped onion

1/2 cup chopped carrot

1/2 cup chopped celery

Salt and freshly ground black pepper

3 quarts chicken broth or stock, homemade or store-bought

1/2 cup wild rice, or wild rice blend

1 head escarole

Juice of 1 to 2 lemons

Directions:

In a large pot on medium-high heat, melt the butter. Add the vegetables and a generous pinch of salt and pepper, and toss to coat. Reduce heat to medium-low, cover pot, and cook for 5 minutes, allowing vegetables to soften without browning. Add broth and wild rice and bring to a boil. Lower heat, partially cover pot, and simmer about 45 minutes, until rice is cooked.

Meanwhile, prep the escarole by trimming off the stem end and chopping the leaves. Wash and dry the escarole in a salad spinner.

Add escarole to the finished soup, stir in a few tablespoons of lemon juice, and add salt and pepper to taste. Add more lemon juice as desired.

ALMOST FLOURLESS CHOCOLATE ALMOND CAKE

Makes: 12 servings   **Total time:** 60 to 70 minutes

Gear: springform pan, measuring cups and spoons, mixing bowls, handheld mixer or stand mixer, mesh sieve, rubber scraper, cooling rack, cake stand

The inspiration for this cake is a fantastic and endlessly adaptable *Bon Appétit* recipe from 1995 called Elodie's Chocolate Cake. This variation is my current fave. It's fancy enough to be a special-occasion dessert, and easy enough to be a no-big-deal, weeknight treat. The texture is rich and cakey, and the chocolate-almond flavor is pitch perfect. It's at its finest served with whipped cream or ice cream on the side.

Ingredients:

1 1/4 cups chocolate chips

2 sticks unsalted butter

5 large eggs

1 1/8 cups sugar

1/2 teaspoon almond extract

1 teaspoon vanilla extract

1/3 cup all-purpose flour

1 1/2 teaspoons baking powder

Pinch of salt

Cocoa powder for garnish

Whipped cream or vanilla ice cream, optional

Directions:

Preheat oven to 325°F. Butter and flour a 10-inch spring-form pan, and set it on a baking sheet. In a glass bowl or large heatproof glass measuring cup, combine the chocolate and butter and heat in the microwave in 15- to 20-second intervals, stirring frequently, until just melted. Set aside.

In the bowl of a stand mixer or in a large bowl using a handheld mixer, beat eggs and sugar until well blended. Add almond and vanilla extracts, and stir to combine. Sift in flour, baking powder, and salt, and stir to combine. Pour in the chocolate mixture, and stir until just combined; transfer the batter to prepared pan.

Bake 20 minutes, then cover pan with foil and continue baking until cake tester comes out clean with moist crumbs, about 30 minutes more. Uncover the cake and leave it in the pan, on a rack, to cool. When ready to serve, run a butter knife around the edge of the pan to loosen cake, then release the springform pan collar.

Place cake on a stand or plate (to keep the springform pan base from slipping around, place a piece of gently crumpled damp paper towel on the stand before placing the cake on it), dust with cocoa powder, and serve with a dollop of whipped cream, if desired.

Cake can be made 1 day ahead and stored covered at room temperature.

CRUMB CAKE MINI MUFFINS

Makes: 16 mini muffins　　**Total time:** 30 minutes

Gear: mini muffin tin, parchment paper mini muffin tin liners, whisk, measuring cups and spoons, mixing bowls, rubber scraper, cooling rack, cake stand

Kids can easily help prep these little two-bite delights. Using a gallon zip-top bag to pipe the batter into the muffin tin holes makes it so easy.

Muffins:

1 cup flour

6 tablespoons granulated sugar

1 teaspoon baking powder

1/4 teaspoon salt

1/2 teaspoon cinnamon

1/4 cup melted butter

1 egg

1/3 cup milk

1 teaspoon vanilla extract

Crumb topping:

1/3 cup all-purpose flour

1/3 cup packed brown sugar

1/3 stick cold butter, cut into small pieces

Pinch of salt

Directions:

Preheat oven to 350°F.

Place liners in 16 mini muffin cups.

To make muffin batter, in a large bowl, whisk together flour, granulated sugar, baking powder, salt, and cinnamon. Add melted butter and stir with a fork until the mixture is crumbly. Add egg, milk, and vanilla, and continue mixing to combine. Batter will have small lumps. Pour (or pipe with a gallon-size zip-top bag with a corner snipped off, or a piping bag) the batter into prepared muffin tin, filling each cup almost to the top, but not all the way.

To make crumb topping, in a small bowl combine flour, brown sugar, butter, and salt. Using your fingers, pinch the mixture together continuously until it achieves a texture resembling small pebbles and sand. Sprinkle a generous pinch on top of each muffin, pressing it slightly into the batter.

Bake for 15 minutes. Cool 10 minutes before removing from muffin tin.

CHECKLIST FOR A
LARGE OR FOREVER HOME KITCHEN

Here's a handy checklist that you can mark up and tear out. It includes all of the must-have gear and pantry essentials for a large or forever home kitchen, so you can keep track of what you have and what you need. I hope this list will make shopping and planning easy.

GEAR

- dinnerware
- flatware
- glassware
- mugs
- chef's knife
- paring knife
- serrated knife
- cutting boards
- nonstick pans
- saucepan with lid
- large pot and stockpot with lids
- rimmed baking sheet
- cooling rack
- baking dishes
- large lightweight bowl
- mixing bowls
- measuring cups and spoons
- glass storage containers with lids

- utensil holder
- vegetable peeler
- box grater
- whisk
- wooden spoon
- spatula
- rubber scraper
- spring-loaded tongs
- ladle
- slotted spoon
- offset spatula
- pepper mill
- corkscrew and can opener
- meat thermometer
- salad spinner
- colander and handheld strainer
- muffin and cupcake tin
- coffee maker and kettle

- coffee grinder
- toaster and/or toaster oven
- kitchen linens
- handheld electric mixer
- blender and food processor
- kitchen shears
- handheld mandoline-style slicer
- potato masher or ricer
- rasp grater
- handheld citrus juicer
- cake and pie pans
- lasagna pan
- stainless steel and/or enameled cast iron cookware and Dutch oven
- wineglasses and bar glasses
- stand mixer

- countertop oven or fancy toaster

- wok

- more sheet pans of different sizes

- seven- or nine-quart enameled round iron Dutch oven

- extra-large, heavy-duty roasting pan

- gravy boat

- waffle maker

- mini muffin tins

- standing citrus press

- immersion blender

- air fryer

- multicooker

- spiralizer

- serving platters, bowls, and utensils

- rolling pin

- cake plate or cake stand

PANTRY ITEMS

- olive oil

- neutral-flavored oil

- nonstick spray

- red or white wine vinegar

- distilled white vinegar

- canned and jarred essentials

- salt (table and kosher) and pepper (or peppercorns for a pepper mill)

- dried herbs and spices

- short and long pasta

- rice

- quinoa or couscous

- coffee and tea

- nuts, nut butters, preserves, and sweeteners
- honey and/or agave syrup
- onion
- garlic
- all-purpose flour
- baking soda
- baking powder
- light brown sugar
- granulated sugar
- vanilla extract
- almond extract
- semisweet chocolate chips
- cocoa powder
- oats
- parchment paper
- condiments
- avocados

- lemons and limes
- ginger
- eggs
- plain yogurt
- butter and cream cheese
- frozen necessities
- more salt options
- anchovies
- Worcestershire sauce
- jarred roasted red peppers
- sherry vinegar
- rice wine vinegar
- toasted sesame oil
- hot sauces
- coconut milk
- Thai curry paste
- miso
- fish sauce

- Spanish paprika
- pumpkin pie spice
- turmeric powder
- cardamom
- coriander
- fennel seeds
- za'atar
- sumac
- tahini
- dried chilis
- chili powder

CONCLUSION

My goal in writing this book has been to leave you feeling empowered and filled with confidence to turn your kitchen into the warm heart of your home. I hope you will fill it with great gear and all the ingredients you need to cook delicious things for yourself, your family, and your friends. I know you'll ace the essential techniques and recipes in this book and be set to take on new ones without trepidation. And last, I hope, with this book in hand, you feel like you have the blueprints and marching orders that were promised at the start to get it all done. After that, all that's left is to step up to the stove, and I know you'll be ready.

ACKNOWLEDGMENTS

A big thank-you to Simon & Schuster and Tiller Press for the opportunity to write this book. In particular, thanks to my editor, Lauren Hummel, for her insightful questions, suggestions, and organizational superpowers, and to Samantha Hoback for getting it all into shape. My appreciation as well to Anja Schmidt, and a special thank-you to Theresa DiMasi for knowing this was the book for me.

I would also like to thank friends, colleagues, fellow cooks, and dining companions for all the good ideas, food talk, and inspiration: Grace Young, Irene Sax, Nancy Hawley, Leslie Fink, Jamie Schneider, Melanie Mannarino, Julie Hartigan (and the rest of my WW crew past and present), Fabio Parasecoli, Pat Gallagher, Gabrielle Lenart, Evie Hantzopoulos, David Motamed, Susanne Sasic, Bill Ryan, Barbara Herring, Regina McLean, Chris Tatti, Yuki Kanaya, Amy Cappellazzo, Alex Patsavas Rosenfeld, Seth Rosenfeld, Helen Pai, Dave Rygalski, Rebecca Harrington, Adam Kaplan, Ira Kaplan, Georgia Hubley, Pat Longo, Alison Lee, Tom Beaujour, Maria McKenna, Laura Foligno, Monica Plotka, Lyn Dexheimer, Joan Enger, Eva Haragova, Shana Lee, Monika Nemeth. And thanks to my CIVIS friends and families, as well as Roberto Lucchini, Andrea Curati, Sara Bevilacqua, and Federica Francisci for the perfect Italian lead-up to this project.

My deepest gratitude to my parents, Carole and Arnold, in particular my mom, for a lifetime of cooking, especially the phenomenal holiday shortbread cookies that probably started all this. And to my brother, David, whose gusto for food made it so fun to hang out in the kitchen—even better with Ciara and Fionn, and Mary Grace Kelly, too. Big thanks to my aunts—Shirley Giallombardo, Cynthia Jainchill, and Wende Tragash—whose kitchens I also grew up in, and still love visiting. And to the rest of my Buffalo family and friends: Nancy, Sussan, Lyla, and Marian Giallombardo, Melissa and Mark Jainchill, Chris, Meagan, Lena, and Dom Evans, Erin Kelly and Charlie von Simson. Also, in memory of my in-laws, Murray and Arlene Hysen, whose beautifully organized kitchens made a huge impression on me—thanks for all the time we spent together cooking and eating, along with Jeff, Sue, Eric, and Dylan Hysen, too.

I am especially grateful to my amazing husband, Lyle Hysen, for the encouragement and support, always, and for being my trusted first reader and editor. Thanks for keeping me laughing, too. A big thank-you, also, to my fabulous daughters, Charlotte and Juliet Hysen, for the valuable suggestions and recipe feedback, and for being my photography and styling dream team. Hazel, the sweetest poodle, thank you for being a constant companion and protecting me from the wolves.

INDEX

ABOUT THE AUTHOR

Lisa Chernick is a native of Buffalo, New York, who fell for food and cooking while living in Italy. She studied at universities in both Rome and Siena, graduated from Boston University, and attended culinary school at New York City's Institute of Culinary Education. Lisa has been a food writer and editor for more than twenty years; from *Food Arts* magazine to the early days of Epicurious and most recently at Weight Watchers' website, cookbooks, and magazine. She has been a James Beard Book Awards judge since 2006 and a James Beard Award nominee herself for digital writing and editing. An avid home cook, Lisa shares her Hoboken, New Jersey, home with her husband, two fabulous daughters, and an exceptional mini poodle.